OXFORD
preparation course
for the TOEIC® test

OXFORD
UNIVERSITY PRESS

OXFORD
UNIVERSITY PRESS

Great Clarendon Street, Oxford OX2 6DP

Oxford University Press is a department of the University of Oxford.
It furthers the University's objective of excellence in research, scholarship,
and education by publishing worldwide in

Oxford New York

Auckland Cape Town Dar es Salaam Hong Kong Karachi
Kuala Lumpur Madrid Melbourne Mexico City Nairobi
New Delhi Shanghai Taipei Toronto

With offices in

Argentina Austria Brazil Chile Czech Republic France Greece
Guatemala Hungary Italy Japan Poland Portugal Singapore
South Korea Switzerland Thailand Turkey Ukraine Vietnam

OXFORD and OXFORD ENGLISH are registered trade marks of
Oxford University Press in the UK and in certain other countries

Photocopying

ISBN-13: 978 0 19 453517 5
ISBN-10: 0-19-453517-7

Printed in China

ACKNOWLEDGEMENTS

*The author and publisher would like to thank the following for their kind
permission to reproduce photographs and other artwork copyright material:*

Cover:
Corbis (cinema exterior), DigitalVision (meeting), Powerstock
(biologist),Stone/Stuart McClaymont (aeroplane).

Alamy p 65 (buskers/Michael Short/Robert Harding), Corbis pp 46
(woman filing), 63 (chef), 64 (friends watching a film), 65
(cinema exterior), 103 (measuring a window), 121 (aeroplanes in
hanger), 140 (steel construction, windmills), 158 (dentist with
patient), 185 (Hong Kong); Digital Vision pp 82 (business
meeting), 83 (television conference); Eyewire p 18 (bottle of
pills); The Image Bank pp 84 (office scene/Henry Sims), 101
(couple with architect/Donata Pizzi), 103 (house painters/Steve
Dunwell Photography), 120 (aeroplane meal/Tom Hussey), 141
(computer/Dag Sundberg), 159 (optical treatment/Harry
Sieplinga, road rage/Yellow Dog Productions), Powerstock pp 139
(biologist), 141 (watch-maker/Zefa-Abril); Photodisc pp 10
(aeroplane, businesspeople), 11 (three businessmen), 12 (chef,
bridge), 14 (three business executives), 15 (pedestrian crossing,
woman on bicycle), 16 (restaurant), 17 (man shopping), 18
(construction site), 19 (busy road), 44 (business meeting), 45
(woman at counter, photocopier room), 46 (women shaking
hands, man and computer), 63 (couple in restaurant), 64 (buying
a ticket), 82 (computer), 84 (business meeting), 101 (house for
sale), 102 (house construction), 103 (carpet installer), 121
(passengers on platform), 122 (ocean liner, teenagers in diner),
160 (couple in bathroom), 178 (two businessmen, waitress), 179
(newspaper), 180 (stock exchange, businesspeople shaking
hands), 181 (presentation, courtyard), 182 (highrise buildings,
businesspeople), 186 (buses), 187 (plumber); Robert Harding
Picture Library pp 46 (man with graphs), 65 (tea at The
Ritz/Adam Woolfitt), 83 (stock exchange), 139 (control panel/Tom
Carroll/Phototake NYC), 160 (man reading newspaper); Stockbyte
pp 11 (man reading newspaper), 19 (executives on train), 179
(man hailing a taxi), 184 (businessman using cell phone), 187
(businesswomen); Stone pp 44 (man writing/Bruce Ayres), 65
(Japanese chef/Charles Gupton), 84 (business seminar/Michael
Rosenfeld, business meeting/Tim Macpherson), 102 (construction
workers), 103 (Japanese sign/Andy Sacks), 120 (captain on
bridge/Christian Lagereek), 122 (airline check-in/Klaus Lahnstein),
141 (clearing rubble/Chip Porter, students in television
studio/Andy Sacks), 158 (businessman leaving aeroplane/Stuart
McClaymont), 160 (doctor with patient/Elie Bernager,
masseuse/Michelangelo Gratton); Telegraph Colour Library p 122
(man riding on a bus/Rob Brimson).

Commissioned photography by:

Emily Anderson p 17 (Designers); Gareth Boden p 14 (Business
man by car); Haddon Davies Photography pp 183 (Leaving
office), 184 (Reception desk); Rob Judges pp 13 (Doctor), 16
(Postroom); Bill Osment p 185 (Train station); O.U.P. pp 13 (Man
at computer), 183 (Dinner table), 186 (Restaurant).

Contents

Introduction

The TOEIC® Test

Before you start studying this book, take a few minutes to read the material on the next few pages. The more you know about the TOEIC, its format, background, and audience, the more comfortable you'll feel when it comes time to take the test.

1 What is the TOEIC?

The Test of English for International Communication (TOEIC) was developed in 1979 by ETS, the same group that developed the Test of English as a Foreign Language (TOEFL).

Since English is one of the most commonly used languages for international commerce, employers saw the need to have a common measure of the language skills of employees and prospective employees. The TOEIC was dcvcloped to assess the English language skills of people around the world working in multinational companies, schools and government organizations.

2 Who takes the TOEIC?

Your employer may ask you for a TOEIC score in order to be promoted or you may have to provide a TOEIC score in order to apply for a certain job. Maybe you are finishing a language program and want to have an official score and certificate to take with you and show your employer, school, family or friends. Whatever your reason, a TOEIC score is recognized around the world.

3 How is the TOEIC different from the TOEFL?

Both the TOEIC and the TOEFL are standardized tests; that is, the scores of test-takers in China are comparable to the scores of test-takers in Argentina. The TOEFL is used primarily for admissions to universities and academic programs in America, while the TOEIC is used primarily for businesses and government organizations. Materials found on the TOEFL come from academic settings; while materials found on the TOEIC come from everyday situations and language in business settings.

4 What kind of English is tested?

Business English covers a very large area. In the TOEIC, the language tested usually falls into one of the following categories.

Offices and Personnel
Entertaining and Dining Out
General Business and Finance
Housing and Property
Travel
Technical Areas
Health and Everyday English

5 What is the format of the test?

Section I	Time	Section II	Time
Listening Comprehension	45 minutes	Reading Comprehension	75 minutes
	Items		Items
Part I	20	Part V	40
Part II	30	Part VI	20
Part III	30	Part VII	40
Part IV	20		
Total Items	100	Total Items	100

6 What is being tested?

Listening Comprehension Section
In the Listening Comprehension Section, you are being tested on your ability to understand spoken English. The listening passage in each part becomes longer moving from one spoken sentence in Part I to a short talk in Part IV.

In Part I, you will see a picture in your test book and hear four short statements. You should choose the statement that best describes the picture.

In Part II, you will hear two speakers. The first speaker will ask a question. You will then hear three possible responses to the question. You should pick the best response.

In Part III, you will hear a short conversation between two people. Then you will read a question in the test booklet about the conversation followed by four responses. You should pick the best response.

In Part IV you will hear a short talk. You will read several questions for each talk followed by four answer choices. You should pick the best response.

Reading Comprehension Section

In the Reading Comprehension Section you are being tested on your ability to understand written English. Your knowledge of vocabulary and grammar is tested as well as your ability to find the answers to questions about details and to identify the main idea of a reading passage.

In Part V you will read an incomplete sentence. There are four answer choices with words or phrases. You should pick the answer choice that best completes the sentence.

In Part VI you will recognize errors. Four words or phrases are underlined in each sentence. You should choose the letter (A, B, C, or D) that contains the error.

In Part VII you will read several passages in the form of letters, articles, notices, forms and advertisements. Several questions will follow each passage. You should choose the one best answer. The best answer is stated or implied in the passage.

7 How do the distractors distract?

In each question of the TOEIC, you will find what we call "distractors". They are used to distract or confuse you. Some of the most common distractors in the Listening Section are:

- similar sounding words (example: *president* is spoken and you read *precedent*).
- a reasonable answer but in the wrong context or situation (example: you see a picture of a plate on a table and the answer choice indicates that the plate is being washed)
- irrelevant answer choices (example: you see a picture of a person buying a radio and an answer choice indicates that the person is purchasing a computer).
- a word in the answer choice is repeated from the question (example: *president* is in the question and is in the answer choice).
- an illogical response (example: the question asks *what* and an answer choice indicates *where*).

In both the Listening Comprehension and Reading Sections, you'll find distractors that:

- repeat a word or make a connection with a word or phrase (example: a passage mentions architecture in San Francisco and an answer choice repeats San Francisco or includes California).
- are reasonable if a key section is misunderstood (example: you hear or read about an employee being honored and the answer choice indicates a birthday party).

Here is some advice to help you avoid choosing attractive distractors:

- Read or listen to the question carefully and make sure the option actually answers the question.
- Read all the answer choices carefully.
- Identify key words that are particular to certain contexts.
- Think of words that could be associated with these key words.
- Ask questions as you listen or read:
    where is this taking place?
    who is involved?
    what is happening?
- Become familiar with parts of speech and word families.

8 TOEIC directions

The directions for each part of the TOEIC are always the same. Become familiar with the directions, so that when you take the official test you don't need to spend time reading the directions.

9 More information

You can get more information about the TOEIC test, TOEIC test dates, and TOEIC worldwide representatives on the TOEIC website http://www.toeic.com

Oxford Preparation for the TOEIC® Course

Now take a few moments to read about this preparation course. You can find out what it consists of and how you can use it to your own particular needs.

1 What is included in this book?

Practice Test 1
Chapter 1   Offices and Personnel
Chapter 2   Entertaining and Dining Out
Chapter 3   General Business and Finance
Chapter 4   Housing and Property
Chapter 5   Travel
Chapter 6   Technical Areas
Chapter 7   Health and Everyday English
Practice Test 2
Grammar Glossary
Sample Answer Sheets
Conversion Table

The Practice Tests

You'll find two complete TOEIC practice tests in this book. There is one at the beginning and one at the end of the book. Each test contains 200 questions. But don't stop there! Taking practice tests isn't enough.

One of the best ways to improve your score on the TOEIC is to study and learn from your mistakes. Explanations to each answer choice and a full tapescript for each question are included in the **Teacher's Book**. Study these explanations to the questions. Why is answer (A) correct and why are answer choices (B), (C) and (D) incorrect? If you can answer these questions, you're on the road to a better score. If you have difficulty in understanding the listening sections, listen and follow the tapescripts to accustom yourself to the type of dialogues you will hear in the TOEIC.

You can use the practice tests in two ways. (1) Take as much time as you need; or (2) do each section in the time allowed on the actual test (see section 5 on page 4 *What is the format of the test?*). It would be a good idea to do at least one of the tests under strict conditions, keeping to the time and not using any aids (dictionary, etc.). You should practice using the **Sample Answer Sheets** (p222 – 223) as you complete the test.

Once you've checked your answers against the key, use the **Conversion Table** (p224) to see your approximate TOEIC score. This score is only an approximate guide and cannot be substituted for an actual TOEIC score. Make a note of the tasks you missed. When you study the seven chapters, pay attention to those particular tasks as they are taught. These will be the areas you should study carefully.

Chapters 1–7

The seven chapters will help you to develop the strategies, skills and vocabulary that are necessary to do well on the test. Each chapter focuses on a context that is emphasized on the TOEIC test (*Offices and Personnel, Entertaining and Dining Out*, etc.). Each chapter is divided into the seven parts of the TOEIC listening and reading sections. Each part contains two strategies and two tasks. Each part makes you aware of the potential traps that are found on the TOEIC test and the strategies you will need to achieve a high score. Each part ends with a review that has test questions just like those on the TOEIC test.
As you study each chapter, think about these tasks. What is the question asking you to do? If you can identify the task, answering the question will be much easier. If you can identify potential traps, answering the question correctly will be very easy.

2 How should I use this book?

Start with Practice Test One. Use the answer key and tapescripts to judge what you know and what you need to focus on.

Pick out the chapters or the parts of chapters that are of interest to you and study them. Pay attention to the strategies that are taught. The strategies focus your attention on the different kinds of questions that may appear in each part of the test. They also highlight the different traps and distractors that are used on the TOEIC. It is important to remember these and be aware of them as you are taking the test. The tasks are designed to improve your vocabulary and increase your level of English.

You must be an active test taker as well as an active learner. Pay attention to how the activities help you understand the tasks. Once you learn to recognize the tasks, you will be able to answer the questions without difficulty. Make this your test-taking strategy and you will achieve a high score on the TOEIC.

3 What if I haven't time to do it all?

This book has been written with that in mind. It is an easy book to dip in and out off. You can focus on those parts of the test that you need to study, and leave the sections that you don't have time for.

Alternatively if there is a topic area that you need to improve on, you may focus on that particular chapter. By doing so, it will help you to improve your vocabulary in that specific business area.

4 What is the Grammar Glossary for?

The grammar glossary has been included to help you to understand fully the strategies and tasks. Grammar terminology is sometimes used in explaining a strategy. A cross reference has been added to the Grammar Glossary, where you will find a brief explanation of the particular language point.

Grammar Glossary **Conjunctions** (p215).

If you feel you need to practice an area of grammar, it is advisable to use an American English or British English grammar reference book.

5 What is the Conversion Table?

A score conversion table is used to convert the number of correctly answered questions into a TOEIC score. The table provides you with an approximation of your total actual score for the practice tests, and can be used to assess how you have improved after completing the chapters. The conversion table converts the score of the practice tests in this book and does not correlate with the actual TOEIC tests.

Practice Test One

Listening Comprehension

In this section of the test, you will have the chance to show how well you understand spoken English. There are four parts to this section, with special directions for each part.

PART I

Directions: For each question, you will see a picture in your test book and you will hear four short statements. The statements will be spoken just one time. They will not be printed in your test book, so you must listen carefully to understand what the speaker says.

When you hear the four statements, look at the picture in your test book and choose the statement that best describes what you see in the picture. Then, on your answer sheet, find the number of the question and mark your answer. Look at the sample below.

Sample Answer
Ⓐ ● Ⓒ Ⓓ

Now listen to the four statements.

Statement (B), "They're having a meeting," best describes what you can see in the picture. Therefore, you should choose answer (B).

GO ON TO THE NEXT PAGE

1.

2.

3.

4.

GO ON TO THE NEXT PAGE ▶

5.

6.

7.

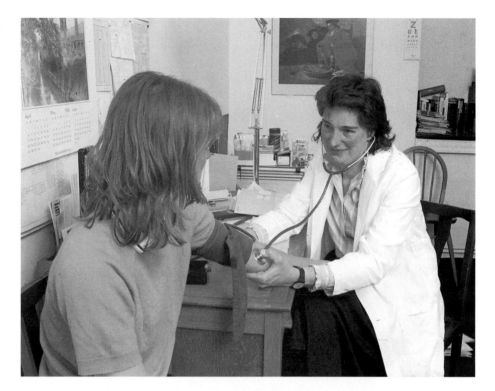

8.

GO ON TO THE NEXT PAGE

9.

10.

11.

12.

GO ON TO THE NEXT PAGE ➤

13.

14.

15.

16.

GO ON TO THE NEXT PAGE

17.

18.

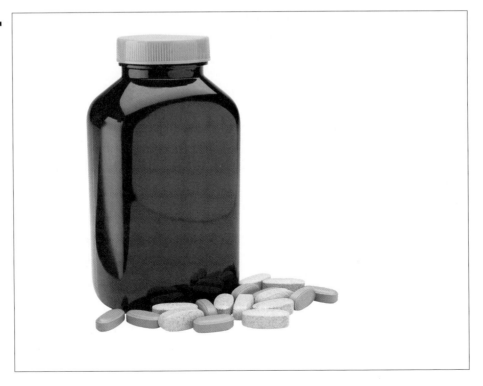

19.

20.

GO ON TO THE NEXT PAGE

PART II

Directions: In this part of the test, you will hear a question spoken in English, followed by three responses, also spoken in English. The question and the responses will be spoken just one time. They will not be printed in your test book, so you must listen carefully to understand what the speakers say. You are to choose the best response to each question.

Now listen to a sample question.

You will hear:

Sample Answer
● Ⓑ Ⓒ

You will also hear:

The best response to the question "How are you?" is choice (A), "I am fine, thank you." Therefore, you should choose answer (A).

21. Mark your answer on your answer sheet.

22. Mark your answer on your answer sheet.

23. Mark your answer on your answer sheet.

24. Mark your answer on your answer sheet.

25. Mark your answer on your answer sheet.

26. Mark your answer on your answer sheet.

27. Mark your answer on your answer sheet.

28. Mark your answer on your answer sheet.

29. Mark your answer on your answer sheet.

30. Mark your answer on your answer sheet.

31. Mark your answer on your answer sheet.

32. Mark your answer on your answer sheet.

33. Mark your answer on your answer sheet.

34. Mark your answer on your answer sheet.

35. Mark your answer on your answer sheet.

36. Mark your answer on your answer sheet.

37. Mark your answer on your answer sheet.

38. Mark your answer on your answer sheet.

39. Mark your answer on your answer sheet.

40. Mark your answer on your answer sheet.

41. Mark your answer on your answer sheet.

42. Mark your answer on your answer sheet.

43. Mark your answer on your answer sheet.

44. Mark your answer on your answer sheet.

45. Mark your answer on your answer sheet.

46. Mark your answer on your answer sheet.

47. Mark your answer on your answer sheet.

48. Mark your answer on your answer sheet.

49. Mark your answer on your answer sheet.

50. Mark your answer on your answer sheet.

PART III

Directions: In this part of the test, you will hear thirty short conversations between two people. The conversations will not be printed in your test book. You will hear the conversations only once, so you must listen carefully to understand what the speakers say.

In your test book, you will read a question about each conversation. The question will be followed by four answers. You are to choose the best answer to each question and mark it on your answer sheet.

51. What does the woman want to do?

    (A) Clean up the papers.
    (B) Close the business for the day.
    (C) Read a section of the newspaper.
    (D) Finish writing the report.

52. Where does the man want to go?

    (A) To the end of the train.
    (B) A suburb of Pittsburgh.
    (C) To the Lost and Found Office.
    (D) To his job.

53. Who is Ellen?

    (A) Wayne's relative.
    (B) Chin's boss.
    (C) A new worker.
    (D) A consultant.

54. Why did the doctor change plans?

    (A) The nurse has a contagious disease.
    (B) He has another operation.
    (C) The problem is more serious than he thought.
    (D) Some hospital employees are protesting.

55. Why is the woman excited?

    (A) Competition among coffee shops is stiff.
    (B) It is hard to locate excellent coffee.
    (C) She ran out of coffee.
    (D) She got a dozen roses and breakfast in bed.

56. Where does the conversation take place?

    (A) In a taxi.
    (B) On a plane.
    (C) On a bus.
    (D) In a car.

57. Why is the man upset?

    (A) More construction would help the area.
    (B) He believes there are enough places to live.
    (C) He is a housing specialist.
    (D) A protest is being organized.

58. Why did the man receive a present?

    (A) It was his birthday.
    (B) He helped his employer.
    (C) It was a prize.
    (D) He cared for some animals.

59. What are the speakers discussing?

    (A) The danger for people who walk.
    (B) The new laws in effect.
    (C) The number of motor vehicles.
    (D) The quality of driving schools.

60. What do the men think about the restaurant?

    (A) It's convenient.
    (B) It's old fashioned.
    (C) It's closing next week.
    (D) It's expensive.

61. What will the man do?

    (A) Order auto parts.
    (B) Bring in his car.
    (C) Get directions to the shop.
    (D) Find out when his car will be ready.

62. Who needs directions?

    (A) Steven.
    (B) Molly.
    (C) Kim.
    (D) The office manager.

GO ON TO THE NEXT PAGE

63. What did the woman do?

    (A) Change her seats.
    (B) Purchase tickets.
    (C) Call her friends.
    (D) Look for the theater.

64. What are the speakers discussing?

    (A) Corporate funding of certain government projects.
    (B) Risky investments.
    (C) The arrival of a new politician.
    (D) A business that is no longer open.

65. Why is there a lunch?

    (A) To welcome two new employees.
    (B) To celebrate Uta and Rachel's promotion.
    (C) To bid farewell to employees.
    (D) To discuss new jobs in the company.

66. What are the men discussing?

    (A) The unpredictable weather.
    (B) The heat this summer.
    (C) The new line of clothes.
    (D) The population of the city.

67. Where does Jean work?

    (A) At a utility company.
    (B) At the City College.
    (C) At a golf course.
    (D) At a publishing house.

68. How do the speakers feel about the new road?

    (A) It should have been built earlier.
    (B) The cost is much too high.
    (C) It will damage the coast.
    (D) They're disappointed.

69. Why didn't the woman know about the meeting?

    (A) She was at lunch at noon.
    (B) She was out of the office nearly all day.
    (C) She already has health insurance.
    (D) She wasn't interested.

70. What will the man do?

    (A) Call Clyde with the information.
    (B) Stay in a historic hotel.
    (C) Look for the name of the place.
    (D) Recommend that Clyde leave Madrid.

71. Where is the conversation taking place?

    (A) At a conference.
    (B) Near Rob's desk.
    (C) In a meeting.
    (D) At a computer store.

72. How do the women know that the plane is late?

    (A) There is always a delay.
    (B) Maggie contacted them.
    (C) Victor called the airline.
    (D) They heard it at the airport.

73. What is the purpose of the plan?

    (A) To create more business.
    (B) To find new employees.
    (C) To save money.
    (D) To motivate the existing clients.

74. What do the men think?

    (A) They should give a presentation.
    (B) The proposal was better last year.
    (C) Sarah's proposals are always accepted.
    (D) It will be rejected again.

75. What is Karl's job?

    (A) He's a scientist.
    (B) He's a reporter.
    (C) He's a salesman.
    (D) He's a mathematician.

76. What does the woman want?

    (A) To set an exact time.
    (B) To pick up some documents.
    (C) To end the negotiation with her lawyers.
    (D) To drive over sooner.

77. What does the woman want the man to do?

    (A) Buy her a car.
    (B) Look at automobiles with her.
    (C) Drive more safely.
    (D) Sell his Volvo.

78. Why are the speakers concerned?

    (A) The company's prices are very high.
    (B) The economy is bad.
    (C) New laws have been made.
    (D) Many businesses are relocating.

79. What is the woman's problem?

    (A) The man isn't a specialist.
    (B) Her computer needs to be fixed.
    (C) She works too slowly.
    (D) She doesn't have a computer.

80. Who is the man talking with?

    (A) A teller.
    (B) A dentist.
    (C) The police.
    (D) A pharmacist.

GO ON TO THE NEXT PAGE

Directions: In this part of the test, you will hear several short talks. Each will be spoken just one time. They will not be printed in your test book, so you must listen carefully to understand and remember what is said.

In your test book, you will read two or more questions about each short talk. The questions will be followed by four answers. You are to choose the best answer to each question and mark it on your answer sheet.

81. Who is speaking?

    (A) An academic researcher.
    (B) A post office employee.
    (C) A new employee.
    (D) A company manager.

82. What will happen next?

    (A) The guests will describe their project.
    (B) They will begin the meeting.
    (C) They will interview the engineers.
    (D) They will eat lunch.

83. For whom is the announcement intended?

    (A) Bus riders.
    (B) Train passengers.
    (C) Maintenance workers.
    (D) Airplane passengers.

84. Why would a listener call extension 142?

    (A) If he is lost.
    (B) If he needs a newspaper.
    (C) If he forgets something.
    (D) If the recycle bins need emptying.

85. What is the speaker doing?

    (A) Making a reservation.
    (B) Checking people into the hotel.
    (C) Giving a tour of the facility.
    (D) Showing the guests the restaurant.

86. What does the speaker recommend?

    (A) A hotel restaurant.
    (B) Tighter security.
    (C) The local historical tour.
    (D) The new movie, *Jane's*.

87. How much money could a listener earn?

    (A) Only $50.
    (B) No more than $100.
    (C) It depends on the number of referrals.
    (D) At least $150.

88. What kind of business is being discussed?

    (A) Telephone service.
    (B) Radio advertising.
    (C) Television programming.
    (D) Newspaper subscription.

89. What is known about the audience?

    (A) They are Visionex customers.
    (B) They have disconnected their service.
    (C) They are qualified salespeople.
    (D) They work for Visionex.

90. Who is speaking?

    (A) A weather reporter.
    (B) A tour guide.
    (C) A coastal resident.
    (D) A state official.

91. When should the situation improve?

    (A) Tonight.
    (B) Tomorrow.
    (C) By Friday.
    (D) On Saturday.

92. How can a listener receive a free phone?

    (A) Mention this ad.
    (B) Sign up within two months.
    (C) Win the grand prize.
    (D) Call their personal service representative.

93. What is unusual about Thomasson Phones?

(A) Owners have their own company representatives.
(B) They can store suggestions.
(C) They come in different colors.
(D) They stay charged for sixty days.

94. Where does this talk take place?

(A) On an airplane.
(B) On a radio program.
(C) At the company headquarters.
(D) In South America.

95. What is Mr. Barral's job?

(A) To attract business to the area.
(B) To build offices.
(C) To start new companies.
(D) To publicize overseas companies.

96. Where does Mr. Barral live now?

(A) In Europe.
(B) In Mexico.
(C) In the Dominican Republic.
(D) In Venezuela.

97. What will happen at the end of the program?

(A) He will talk to panelists.
(B) He will return to VenOil Company.
(C) He will return to Europe.
(D) He will answer questions from listeners.

98. What is the purpose of the talk?

(A) To welcome Ms. Perkins.
(B) To announce the closing of the company.
(C) To introduce the new president.
(D) To open a new office.

99. Who is listening to the talk?

(A) The transportation industry.
(B) The company employees.
(C) Tara Perkins' family.
(D) The summer workers.

100. When will the change take place?

(A) Immediately.
(B) In five quarters.
(C) At the end of the week.
(D) At the beginning of the year.

This is the end of the Listening Comprehension portion of Practice Test One. Turn to Part V in your test book.

GO ON TO THE NEXT PAGE

YOU WILL HAVE ONE HOUR AND FIFTEEN MINUTES TO COMPLETE PARTS V, VI AND VII OF THE TEST.

Reading

In this section of the test, you will have a chance to show how well you understand written English. There are three parts to this section, with special directions for each part.

PART V

Directions: Questions 101–140 are incomplete sentences. Four words or phrases, marked (A), (B), (C), (D) are given beneath each sentence. You are to choose the **one** word or phrase that best completes the sentence. Then, on your answer sheet, find the number of the question and mark your answer.

You will read:

Because the equipment is very delicate,
it must be handled with ....

(A) caring
(B) careful
(C) care
(D) carefully

Sample Answer

(A) (B) ● (D)

The sentence should read, "Because the equipment is very delicate, it must be handled with care." Therefore, you should choose answer (C).

Now begin work on the questions.

---

101. The .... will begin next week in Athens.

(A) conduct
(B) congregation
(C) convenience
(D) convention

102. The financial advisors have .... started their meetings and will continue through the morning.

(A) yet
(B) already
(C) however
(D) still

103. Sue was .... for her dedication to the project and the company.

(A) commanded
(B) predicted
(C) agreed to
(D) praised

104. The air quality has improved, ... it still has a long way to go.

(A) although
(B) than
(C) while
(D) so that

105. The group of .... didn't stop working until 5:00 in the morning.

(A) lawyers
(B) law
(C) lawyer
(D) laws

106. The difference .... the pressure inside and outside the plane is what affects your ears.

(A) between
(B) with
(C) of
(D) on

107. Although her speech was very .... , many found it too long.

(A) interested
(B) interest
(C) interestingly
(D) interesting

108. The World Games have become more popular than .... ever imagined.

(A) everyone
(B) anyone
(C) someone
(D) no one

109. The .... of the passengers will get off at the next station.

(A) major
(B) most
(C) more
(D) majority

110. .... conditions couldn't be asked for to start construction.

(A) Best
(B) Better
(C) Goodly
(D) Well

111. Shoe designers have always looked toward Milan for their ....

(A) inspired
(B) inspirational
(C) inspiration
(D) inspire

112. The city has based its .... estimates primarily on the service industry.

(A) growth
(B) grows
(C) grew
(D) grown

113. The new accountant will be doing .... work that Mr. Drake has been doing.

(A) same as
(B) the same
(C) same
(D) the same as

114. Min left a message for .... boss that she would arrive an hour late.

(A) herself
(B) hers
(C) her
(D) she

115. The account executives were unable to .... on a strategic plan.

(A) agreement
(B) agreed
(C) agree
(D) agrees

116. Cruise One is offering a .... fare for any first-time customers.

(A) reduce
(B) reduces
(C) reduction
(D) reduced

117. Taxi drivers .... the city increase their prices during the tourist season.

(A) on
(B) around
(C) over
(D) under

118. Investors watched the market .... to see how it would react to the unemployment situation.

(A) nearly
(B) tightly
(C) widely
(D) closely

GO ON TO THE NEXT PAGE

119. Kyle was .... busy that he forgot to cancel his dentist appointment.

(A) too
(B) very
(C) so
(D) than

120. The board members are .... to elect a new chairman at the May meeting.

(A) timed
(B) arranged
(C) scheduled
(D) planned

121. A reminder was sent .... all personnel regarding the revised schedule.

(A) to
(B) from
(C) at
(D) on

122. Ms. Kim requested that we order more food for the .... meeting.

(A) next
(B) follow
(C) then
(D) after

123. Employees are encouraged to .... local seminars and workshops.

(A) attending
(B) attended
(C) attend
(D) attendees

124. .... the group has made large contributions, it feels excluded from the community.

(A) So
(B) Even though
(C) However
(D) In spite of

125. All volunteers are .... to arrive thirty minutes before the event.

(A) reviewed
(B) released
(C) requested
(D) resigned

126. .... people than expected left the city on the holiday weekend.

(A) Fewer
(B) Less
(C) The least
(D) Little

127. In preparation for the world premiere, the orchestra is .... twice a day.

(A) practice
(B) practiced
(C) practices
(D) practicing

128. The community is attempting to restore the island to its .... state.

(A) natures
(B) nature
(C) naturally
(D) natural

129. All new orders are on hold .... the defect can be fixed.

(A) until
(B) after
(C) as
(D) only

130. More wine was exported in the third quarter .... in any previous quarter.

(A) that
(B) than
(C) as
(D) then

131. .... show that there will be a shortage of university professors by the end of the decade.

(A) Investigation
(B) Questions
(C) Studies
(D) Proposals

132. Club members should .... their monthly dues on the first of the month.

(A) paid
(B) pay
(C) pays
(D) paying

133. Ebrahim came into the office on Saturday and Sunday and he .... wasn't able to finish the project on time.

(A) still
(B) even
(C) however
(D) although

134. Performances at the Shakespeare Festival begin in June and run .... the end of August.

(A) until
(B) on
(C) just
(D) by then

135. Government agencies are being pressured to conduct .... more like the private sector.

(A) its
(B) themselves
(C) their
(D) itself

136. Neither cameras .... recording devices will be permitted at the board meeting.

(A) neither
(B) or
(C) not
(D) nor

137. The company was saved .... bankruptcy by a multi-million dollar contract with a Middle Eastern firm.

(A) for
(B) with
(C) from
(D) by

138. Airline ticket .... fell when the major airlines implemented their new pricing plans.

(A) sales
(B) sell
(C) sails
(D) sold

139. The product .... will begin as soon as the client has approved the design.

(A) developing
(B) development
(C) developed
(D) develop

140. Ms. Takahashi gave her assistant an .... end-of-the year review.

(A) eager
(B) outstanding
(C) open
(D) initiate

GO ON TO THE NEXT PAGE

PART VI

Directions: In **Questions 141–160**, each sentence has four words or phrases underlined. The four underlined parts of the sentence are marked (A), (B), (C), (D). You are to identify the **one** underlined word or phrase that should be corrected or rewritten. Then, on your answer sheet, find the number of the question and mark your answer.

Example:

All <u>employee</u> are required <u>to wear</u> their
     A   B

<u>identification</u> badges <u>while</u> at work.
    C   D

Sample Answer
● Ⓑ Ⓒ Ⓓ

The underlined word "employee" is not correct in this sentence. This sentence should read, "All employees are required to wear their identification badges while at work." Therefore, you should choose answer (A).

Now begin work on the questions.

---

141. To everyone's <u>surprise</u>, the politician <u>announces</u>
             A   B
her <u>running</u> mate at a press <u>conference</u> last
    C   D
night.

142. <u>Construction</u> on the building <u>is</u> ahead of
     A   B
schedule <u>due to</u> the <u>season</u> weather.
       C   D

143. As <u>an incentive</u>, teachers are not <u>required</u> to
      A   B
pay <u>interest</u> on a new <u>home loaner</u>.
    C   D

144. <u>Unfortunately</u>, <u>the move</u> was <u>put up</u> until early fall
     A   B   C
due to the high <u>rental</u> prices.
           D

145. Dr. Dixon <u>was never able</u> to get <u>in</u> the <u>loss</u> of his
            A   B   C
first heart transplant <u>patient</u>.
           D

146. <u>However</u> they are <u>urgently needed</u>, <u>repairs</u> to the
    A   B   C
bus lines won't be made <u>this</u> year.
              D

147. We <u>don't recommend</u> <u>spend</u> a lot of time <u>making</u>
        A   B   C
changes <u>to the format</u>.
      D

148. <u>Even though</u> Ms. Jones <u>received</u> a raise, she has
     A   B
<u>fewer</u> money <u>than</u> before.
   C   D

149. The earnings report <u>were</u> <u>expected</u> to be
                            A   B
<u>released</u> after the second quarter <u>ended</u>.
  C   D

150. <u>Instability</u> in the government <u>has led</u> to a <u>lower</u>
    A   B   C
in the <u>growth rate</u> of the economy.
         D

151. <u>In addition</u>, the metro <u>runs</u> from the airport <u>onto</u>
     A   B   C
the city center <u>every fifteen minutes</u>.
               D

152. <u>In spite of</u> the <u>weather conditioning</u>, the concert
      A   B
<u>was held</u> in the park <u>as planned</u>.
  C   D

153. <u>Most of</u> the new furniture <u>it</u> was <u>purchased</u> at the
   A   B   C
<u>annual</u> trade fair.
  D

154. The <u>troubled</u> health care organization <u>declined</u>
       A   B
service to <u>more that</u> 500 patients in the last
           C
month <u>alone</u>.
        D

155. The new <u>managers</u> <u>gathered at</u> a mountain
            A   B
retreat <u>to plan</u> <u>his</u> strategy.
        C   D

156. <u>The cause</u> of the fire was <u>never</u> determined, <u>ever</u>
    A   B   C
human error <u>is suspected</u>.
           D

157. Shoppers rushed into the store <u>as soon</u> it opened
                              A
<u>to reach</u> the <u>discounted</u> items <u>before</u> they were
   B   C   D
gone.

158. The accident <u>came as a shock</u> to <u>they</u> who
               A   B
<u>knew about</u> the <u>airline's</u> safety record.
   C   D

159. <u>Because</u> the workers <u>accept</u> a pay cut, they may
    A   B
find <u>themselves</u> <u>without</u> jobs.
       C   D

160. The <u>German</u> telecommunications company is
      A
very <u>interesting</u> in <u>acquiring</u> a small <u>Canadian</u>
       B   C   D
company.

GO ON TO THE NEXT PAGE ▶

PART VII

Directions: Questions 161–200 are based on a selection of reading materials, such as notices, letters, forms, newspaper and magazine articles, and advertisements. You are to choose the **one** best answer (A), (B), (C) or (D) to each question. Then, on your answer sheet, find the number of the question and mark your answer. Answer all questions following each reading selection on the basis of what is **stated** or **implied** in that section.

Read the following example.

The Museum of Technology is a "hands-on" museum, designed for people to experience science at work. Visitors are encouraged to use, test, and handle the objects on display. Special demonstrations are scheduled for the first and second Wednesdays of each month at 13:30. Open Tuesday–Friday 12:00–16:30, Saturday 10:00–17:30, and Sunday 11:00–16:30.

When during the month can visitors see special demonstrations?

Sample Answer
Ⓐ ● Ⓒ Ⓓ

(A)   Every weekend
(B)   The first two Wednesdays
(C)   One afternoon a week
(D)   Every other Wednesday

The reading selection says that the demonstrations are scheduled for the first and second Wednesdays of the month. Therefore, you should choose answer (B).

Now begin work on the questions.

Questions 161–162 refer to the following advertisement.

Are you looking for a job?

Employers from around the country are interested in talking with you! We have gathered over 100 companies, representing a variety of industries, to meet with you at the SELEX JOB FAIR on Saturday and Sunday, May 7–8, from 9:00 a.m. to 4:00 p.m.

Location: Harrisburg City Convention Center
                   105 River Road
                   Building A

Parking is available. No registration is necessary. Bring copies of your resume. For more details, call our Pittsburgh office at 717-999-0077.

---

161. What should interested readers do?

(A) Send the employers their resumes
(B) Call to register
(C) Go to the fair
(D) Check the website

162. Where will the fair be held?

(A) At the employer's office
(B) At a meeting center in Harrisburg
(C) At locations around the country
(D) In Pittsburgh

On Saturday, August 15, volunteers from your local Cancer Research Society will be collecting donations. We welcome any items, particularly furniture, electronics and household goods. If you would like to donate items, please leave them by your front door.

The pick-up schedule is as follows:

Saturday, August 15	Area Between
8 – 10 a.m.	Lincoln and Washington Blvds.
9 – 11 a.m.	Main and Coast Streets.
12 – 2 p.m.	Gregory Blvd. and Laurel Dr.
2 – 4 p.m.	17th and 20th St.
4 – 6 p.m.	Powell Ave. and Brannan Blvd.

If you have any questions, please call 888-535-1212.

163. What is the purpose of the event?

(A) To sell new furniture
(B) To introduce local people to a new organization
(C) To conduct research
(D) To gather used goods

164. Which area has the latest pick-up?

(A) 17th and 20th Streets
(B) Lincoln Blvd. and Coast St.
(C) Brannan and Gregory Blvds.
(D) Powell Ave. and Brannan Blvd.

165. Which items is the society specifically looking for?

(A) Tables and chairs
(B) Clothes
(C) Scientific instruments
(D) Food

GO ON TO THE NEXT PAGE

Memorandum

To: All Staff
From: Jost Rames
RE: Computer Update
Date: March 30

As you know, all employees will receive new computers during May. In order to minimize work disruption, we will be installing the computers over a period of three weeks, rather than all at once, as originally planned. Installation of new computers will be made per department (see schedule, attached). Between now and your scheduled date, you should make copies of all necessary documents and store them on a disk.

We understand that saving files will take planning and time. Each department head has scheduled a two hour work period for employees to go through and save files. If you have any questions or need help with large files, contact me immediately. This is a major investment by the company which will enable all of us to work more efficiently and effectively.

---

166. When will the computers be installed?

(A) During a pre-scheduled, two-hour time slot
(B) All at once
(C) Over several weeks
(D) In March

167. What is the purpose of this page of the memo?

(A) To announce the new purchase
(B) To inform workers of the schedule
(C) To change the leaders of each area
(D) To eliminate unnecessary work

168. What should employees do now?

(A) Create a schedule
(B) Transfer necessary information
(C) Call Mr. Rames
(D) Choose the computer they want

Questions 169–171 refer to the following article.

Sources report that the Dasco Oil Refinery will be closed down by the end of the year. The refinery, located in Davenford, has experienced safety problems. Two explosions occurred last month, causing one injury and an estimated $10 million in damages. In January, a leak was detected by a worker. Production was stopped for 24 hours, causing a temporary oil shortage in the northwest.

There has been no official word from the company headquarters in Dallas. The State Safety Board is leading an investigation and is scheduled to issue a report on Friday. ∎

169. Where does the information come from?

(A) Workers
(B) The Safety Board
(C) The company headquarters
(D) Unnamed individuals

170. Where is the refinery's main office?

(A) In Davenford
(B) In Dasco
(C) In Dallas
(D) North of the site

171. What were the results of the accidents?

(A) The area had no oil.
(B) An employee was fired.
(C) The Safety Board is being investigated.
(D) One person was hurt.

Questions 172–173 refer to the following fax.

EastWest Airlines

1440 Treat Lane
San Diego, CA 90007

July 10, 2002
Mr. Scott Baer
22 Armstrong Dr.
San Francisco, CA 94555

Thank you for choosing EastWest Airlines. The ticket for your flight from San Francisco (SFO) to Philadelphia (PHL) and returning with a connection flight through Chicago (ORD) is being sent to you overnight via mail. The itinerary is:

Mon.	9/20	LV	SFO	FL# EW945 10:23 A
Mon.	9/20	AR	PHL	5:50 P
Fri.	9/24	LV	PHL	FL# EW890 3:45 P
Fri.	9/24	AR	ORD	5:00 P
Fri.	9/24	LV	ORD	FL# EW202 7:30 P
Fri.	9/24	AR	SFO	9:00 P

Seat assignments will be made one week before the scheduled flight.

172. What is the flight number from Chicago?

(A) 945
(B) 730
(C) 890
(D) 202

173. When will Mr. Baer receive his ticket?

(A) Today
(B) On September 20th
(C) Tomorrow
(D) 7 days before the flight

GO ON TO THE NEXT PAGE

Professional Trainers Society Meeting

PTS, the Professional Trainers Society, will hold its monthly meeting on Wednesday at 6:00 p.m. Well-known lecturer and trainer Lyle Hayes will be the guest speaker. His talk is entitled "Incorporating New Technology In Our Training." Everyone is welcome. There is no fee for members; non-members are asked to contribute $10. PTS is a local chapter of the national organization. Meetings are held the third Wednesday of each month.

Agenda

6:00 – 6:30	Socializing	Meet other members
6:30 – 7:00	Chapter Business	President McPhee will lead the meeting
7:00 – 8:30	Key Speaker – Lyle Hayes	Incorporating New Technology
8:30 – 8:45	Question & Answer	
8:45 – 9:00	Upcoming Events / New Business	

174. For whom is the notice written?

(A) Anyone interested in attending
(B) An important speaker
(C) Only current members
(D) The head of the organization

175. Who is Lyle Hayes?

(A) The head of PTS
(B) A member of the organization
(C) An author
(D) A famous speaker

176. What will happen after the talk?

(A) A new president will be elected.
(B) The audience can ask questions.
(C) Mr. Hayes will autograph books.
(D) Food and drinks will be served.

Questions 177–180 refer to the following instructions.

Enclosed you will find your new "First Bank" Automatic Bank Card. Follow these simple instructions to activate it.

- Call the telephone number on the back of the card and press #1. State your full name as it appears on the card. You will then be asked for your city of birth for identification purposes. Upon answering, you will be prompted to enter a four-digit secret identification password. You are encouraged to select a non-obvious password. You will then be asked to repeat it. A representative will confirm your account number. Now, you're ready to use your bank card.

- Please keep the card in a secure place and do not give your password to anyone. At any time, you can call the telephone number if you lose your card or want to change your password.

FIRST BANK

177. For whom are these instructions written?

(A) Bank representatives
(B) New bank customers
(C) A security company
(D) Credit card holders

178. What information will <u>not</u> be asked?

(A) Your birth date
(B) Your account number
(C) Your birthplace
(D) A personal ID number

179. If your birthday is 09/14, what would be the best password for you?

(A) 0914
(B) 013948
(C) Your telephone number
(D) 6952

180. When can customers use the card?

(A) Immediately
(B) When they receive confirmation in the mail
(C) After paying a fee
(D) As soon as they make the phone call

GO ON TO THE NEXT PAGE

Questions 181–184 refer to the following letter.

Drake's Grill
10 Cold Water Canyon
Anchorage, AK 75331

Anchorage Seafood
Route 5
Anchorage, AK 75332

Dear Mr. Blake:

It's with great disappointment that I am writing this letter. We have bought seafood from your company for the last five years. We have always been extremely pleased with the quality and service. That is until now.

Last Friday, we were scheduled to receive our order of 100 pounds of shrimp and 150 pounds of crab at 9:00 a.m. Finally, at 11:30 a.m., your delivery truck arrived, giving us only 30 minutes to prepare for our lunch time crowd. Unfortunately, that wasn't the only problem. The order contained half of what we ordered, and most of the shrimp was bad. We had to change our menu at the last minute, and, as you can imagine, we had many unhappy customers.

We will not pay for this order and are seriously considering another vendor. It is only because we have been buying from you for so long that we want to hear your explanation. You can contact me at the restaurant.

Sincerely

Joanne Brown

Joanne Brown
Manager

181. Why did Ms. Brown write the letter?

(A) To return the food
(B) To express her displeasure with the company
(C) To praise their service
(D) To change the delivery time

182. What was not a problem?

(A) The time of delivery
(B) The amount of seafood
(C) The attitude of the driver
(D) The quality of the product

183. How much shrimp did the restaurant receive?

(A) 50 pounds
(B) 75 pounds
(C) 100 pounds
(D) 150 pounds

184. What does Ms. Brown want to happen next?

(A) She wants Mr. Blake to call her.
(B) She wants Anchorage Seafood to return the money.
(C) She wants to search for a new vendor.
(D) She wants the seafood to be delivered earlier.

38 PRACTICE TEST ONE

Questions 185–186 refer to the following notice.

Following the City Council's unanimous decision on Friday, the new pollution emission charge will go into effect on Tuesday at midnight. The new fee will be 0.25% of a car's current value, and 0.5% of a truck's current value. All residents must pay the fee before the end of the year. The money collected will be used for the Clean Air Program. There are exceptions for low-income households. An information booklet is available at the city office on Pine Street.

---

185. To whom does this notice apply?

(A) People who purchase vehicles after midnight on Tuesday
(B) Vehicle owners who live in the state
(C) Low-income individuals only
(D) Most car and truck owners

186. When does the program begin?

(A) The following day
(B) At the end of the year
(C) Next Tuesday
(D) After the council takes a vote

Questions 187–188 refer to the following article.

Non-profit agencies around the city demonstrated today in front of Brisco Services. Over 100 people took part in the planned event to express their frustration at high property prices. They claim that large companies, which are able to pay skyrocketing rents, are pushing real estate prices out of control. Community service organizations and other non-profit groups, who often aren't able to pay the rents, may be forced to leave the city. They warn that they won't be able to provide the necessary services to those people who need them the most. The agencies are asking some of the most profitable companies to work with them in developing creative solutions. The agencies claim that their services benefit Brisco and the community.

---

187. Which organizations are upset?

(A) Big corporations
(B) The city government
(C) The customer service industry
(D) Those that help citizens

188. Why did the agencies demonstrate?

(A) Property is too expensive
(B) To get funding from Brisco
(C) Brisco controls them
(D) The community isn't interested in their services

GO ON TO THE NEXT PAGE

Questions 189–190 refer to the following instructions.

Follow these simple instructions to purchase or increase value of a multi-transit pass.

1) To buy a new pass, insert coins or bills into the upper left slot. As you insert money, the total will appear in the window. Indicate the amount that you would like to purchase by pushing the up or down arrow. Push the "Ticket" button, take the ticket and your change.

2) If you have a pass and would like to add money to it, insert the pass into the machine. The window will indicate the value of the pass. Insert money until you have added the desired amount. Then push the "Ticket" button and remove the ticket.

Passes are good on all city trains and buses. Prices between destinations are listed on the back of these instructions.

189. How do passengers know the value of their current pass?

(A) It is on the back of the instructions.
(B) It appears on a screen.
(C) It is written on it.
(D) The bus driver tells them.

190. What is true about the passes?

(A) Passengers need exact change.
(B) Passes are only sold in $5 amounts.
(C) Passengers can put additional money on a pass.
(D) They are only valid on the train.

Questions 191–193 refer to the following letter.

112 Barrington Drive
Los Angeles, CA 90043
August 7, 2001

Anh Nguyen
INVESTESE
987 San Gabriel Way
San Diego, CA 93445

Dear Ms. Nguyen:

I met with Lori Uzark last week in San Francisco and she suggested that I contact you. I recently completed a master's degree in business administration here in Los Angeles. I received a job offer from an investment banking firm in my home city of Seoul, Korea. I was ready to return to Korea when I had the good fortune of seeing Lori.

We had lunch and she told me about the exciting work that you and your group are doing. Lori and I met during my first year of business school when we developed a proposal and feasibility study for electronic education offering investment seminars, workshops and classes. We received quite a bit of interest in the proposal.

After speaking with Lori, I knew that I had to speak with you. She mentioned that you are hiring staff. As I mentioned, I have a job offer, but because I am so interested in the work that you are doing, I would like to explore opportunities. I would like to invite you to dinner or to arrange a meeting at your convenience. I will give you a call next week to see if we can arrange something.

Sincerely,
Sun Hee Kang
Sun Hee Kang

191. What is the purpose of the letter?

(A) To submit a proposal
(B) To accept a job offer
(C) To arrange a meeting
(D) To reschedule a job interview

192. Where did Ms. Kang complete her education?

(A) San Diego
(B) Los Angeles
(C) Seoul
(D) San Francisco

193. How did Sun Hee obtain Ms. Nguyen's name?

(A) Her friend Lori gave it to her.
(B) She works for the investment company in Korea.
(C) She did a project for her.
(D) They went to school together.

All packages must be weighed and registered. Scales are located in the warehouse. Staff are available to help you from 6:00 a.m. to 3:00 p.m. The weight and dimensions (length x height x width) for each package must be taken and noted in the registry. Weigh the package only when it is closed and ready to be shipped. This registry is our final record of what has been shipped from the facility. It is of utmost importance that this record is accurate.

194. Why are packages weighed and measured?

(A) To determine the fee for shipping
(B) To determine if they meet the limit
(C) To make note in the registry
(D) To select the proper strapping tape

195. What should senders do first?

(A) Open the package
(B) Write the height and length
(C) Close the package
(D) Weigh the materials

Questions 196–197 refer to the following article.

THE AREA'S LARGEST supermarket chain was ordered to pay $100 million to twenty ex-employees. The court found Acre Foods guilty of racial discrimination. The case began two years ago when minority employees complained that they weren't being promoted. Instead, less experienced white workers received promotions in over twenty separate cases. The employees went to management with their concerns. When no action was taken, they contacted legal representation. Ten of the twenty workers lost their jobs within a month of filing complaints. The other ten workers left the company voluntarily. Each worker will receive $5 million. Acre Foods was unavailable for comment.

196. Why will the workers receive money?

(A) Acre Foods treated them unfairly.
(B) They were promoted.
(C) The company feels that they deserve it.
(D) They need to cover medical costs.

197. What is true about all of the ex-employees?

(A) They are white.
(B) All of them were fired.
(C) They had experience.
(D) They never explained the situation to the management.

Questions 198–200 refer to the following letter.

Embark Industries
10 High Street
Glasgow, Scotland
June 1, 2001

Embark Industries
14-B Rua Barrostos
São Paulo, Brazil

Dear Harriet,

I'm taking this opportunity to finalize our plans for July. As you know, we have hired ten new sales managers. As part of their training, we feel it is essential that they visit at least three of our factories. We also want them to meet local representatives and, when possible, satisfied customers.

With two factories in Brazil, we thought it would be perfect to send the group first to Belo Horizonte and then to São Paulo. Roberto Giostri would be a fine sales representative for them to meet. His English is excellent and he has been one of our most successful representatives for the past five years.

What I would like to ask you is to arrange for the group to meet some customers. They will be in Brazil from July 10–18. If you send me some possible dates, I'll organize the rest of their trip around that. I've already contacted Roberto and the factories. I'll make hotel reservations once I have heard from you. Attached are their flight itineraries. Please contact me as soon as you have any information.

Yours truly,

Rachel

198. Why is Rachel contacting Harriet?

(A) To introduce her to the new managers
(B) To plan her trip to Brazil
(C) To thank her for her help
(D) To ask for some assistance

199. What is their relationship?

(A) Harriet is Rachel's customer.
(B) Harriet works for the competition.
(C) They work for the same company.
(D) Rachel is Harriet's boss in Brazil.

200. What will the sales managers not do while in Brazil?

(A) Negotiate a new deal
(B) Tour a factory
(C) Talk with clients
(D) Meet with a Brazilian employee

Stop! This is the end of the test. If you finish before one hour and fifteen minutes have passed, you may go back to Parts V, VI, and VII and check your work.

Listening comprehension PART I

Strategy A

Use the pictures to identify an event.
Ask yourself *what* is taking place and *where* it is taking place.

What?   The group is having a meeting.
Where?   They are sitting around a table.

What?   The man is filling out a form.
Where?   He's standing at a counter.

Task A

Identify an event

Cross out the words or phrases that do NOT describe the event listed.

1 interview   asking questions, inviting the public, answering, trying to impress, turning up the heat, giving background information

2 recruiting fair networking, applicants, trusted employee, presentation of new products, curriculum vitae, social event

3 office tour   department locations, cafeteria, sightseeing, supply catalogue, parking facilities, off-site drilling

4 training   new employees, human resource regulations, public transportation, rating, mandatory, autonomy

5 promotion   honor, bad track record, praise, special sale, raise, extra inventory

Strategy B

Be aware of prepositions of location. The TOEIC® test often uses prepositions of location (*in*, *on*, *under*, *beneath*, etc.) with words found in the picture. These prepositions could also be used with words associated with the context of the picture, but in different locations.

Compare the statements below that identify the correct location with the other options.

(A) She's resting *at* her desk.
(B) She's standing *by* the fountain.
(C) She's working *behind* the counter.
(D) She's taking flowers *from* the shelves.

The correct answer is (C).

(A) She's ordering more paper *from* the store.
(B) She's standing *by* the copy machine.
(C) She's adding more pages *to* the report.
(D) She's waiting *next to* the door.

The correct answer is (B).

Grammar Glossary Prepositions of Location (p218)

Task B 📼

Identify the location

Listen to the sentences. Check the letter that uses a preposition to describe where something is located.

6   (A) ....✓......   9   (A) ....
    (B) ....   (B) ....

7   (A)   10   (A) ....
    (B) ....   (B) ....

8   (A) ....
    (B) ....

Review

Directions: Listen to the statements and choose the one that best describes what you see in the picture.

11

12

13

14
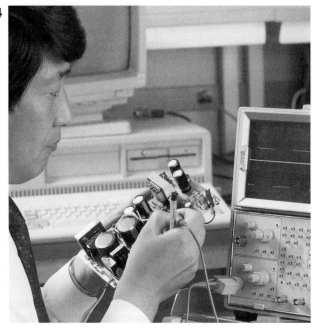

Listening Comprehension

Part I				
11	Ⓐ	Ⓑ	Ⓒ	Ⓓ
12	Ⓐ	Ⓑ	Ⓒ	Ⓓ
13	Ⓐ	Ⓑ	Ⓒ	Ⓓ
14	Ⓐ	Ⓑ	Ⓒ	Ⓓ

PART II

Grammar Glossary **Adjectives: Descriptive Phrases** (p212)

Task A

Identify characteristics

Cross out the answer choices that do NOT answer the question. Underline the adjectives and descriptive phrases in the answer choices.

1. How was the interview with the candidate for the director's job?
   - (A) A little rough at first, and then it improved.
   - (B) ~~The director is very well-respected.~~
   - (C) I can't believe how well we got along.

2. What are you trying to accomplish in the training?
   - (A) Everything was finished by 10:00 a.m.
   - (B) The trainees should leave with a clear idea of the company's mission.
   - (C) Her accomplishments are too many to list.

3. What should be included in an effective memo?
   - (A) Above all, it should be short and concise.
   - (B) He responded to it immediately.
   - (C) A good speaker.

4. What did you include in the job advertisement?
   - (A) The minimum requirements were clearly stated.
   - (B) We received over 200 responses.
   - (C) Everything except for the salary.

5. How do they decide if someone is granted a leave of absence?
   - (A) A valid reason is the top priority.
   - (B) It isn't even considered if you haven't been with the company for over a year.
   - (C) We will truly miss them around the office.

6. What makes her such an excellent speaker?
   - (A) Clarity and enthusiasm.
   - (B) She receives over five requests a week.
   - (C) She truly understands her audience.

7. How are the two committees different?
   - (A) They will both meet tomorrow at 3:00.
   - (B) One is very well-organized.
   - (C) Dave's meetings last more than three hours.

8. What is the annual company party like?
   - (A) Every year they renew the contract.
   - (B) Honestly, it isn't very much fun, but I feel obligated to go.
   - (C) Many employees feel that it is a good way to get to know each other.

9. How is the new database working?
   - (A) It was only installed last month.
   - (B) Every day it becomes more manageable.
   - (C) Employees are finding it very flexible.

10. How well is her replacement doing the job?
    - (A) Clients have been registering quite a few complaints.
    - (B) Extremely well, considering the challenges.
    - (C) The woman has an MBA and a law degree.

Real Spoken English
There are many ways to ask someone to describe something.
Tell me about it, and *What's it like?* are very common. *Can you describe it?* is more formal.

Strategy B

Listen for words that tell you something happens frequently.

> He goes to the gym *every day* after work.
> She doesn't *let a day pass* without her afternoon coffee.
> They are *constantly* advertising for new managers.
> This company is *always* calling emergency meetings.

Grammar Glossary Adverbs: Frequency Words (p213)

Task B

Identify a frequent action

Mark the sentences that indicate a frequent event with an *F*. Mark the sentences that indicate an occasional event with an *O*. Then, underline the word or expression which gave you the answer.

11 (A) He never arrives on time. ..F......
   (B) The meetings are always longer than stated. ..F......
   (C) They occasionally meet after everyone has gone home. ..O......

12 (A) Without fail, the new employees are shocked at the amount of paperwork to be filled out. ....
   (B) Once in a while employees need to file reports. ....
   (C) What was once a monthly occurrence has now turned into a daily routine. ....

13 (A) Every day they pile on more and more responsibilities. ....
   (B) From time to time, every person in the office is expected to help. ....
   (C) All employees are required to assist at least once a month. ....

14 (A) Now that she has started, she can't stop sending out surveys. ....
   (B) You won't have to answer the questions more than a handful of times. ....
   (C) We receive the questionnaire several times a year. ....

15 (A) Part of your daily job responsibilities is to take the messages. ....
   (B) You may be asked on occasion to take messages for the president. ....
   (C) She always returns my message the same day. ....

Review 📼

Directions: Listen and choose the best response to each question.

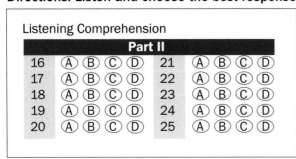

Listening Comprehension		
Part II		
16 Ⓐ Ⓑ Ⓒ Ⓓ	21 Ⓐ Ⓑ Ⓒ Ⓓ	
17 Ⓐ Ⓑ Ⓒ Ⓓ	22 Ⓐ Ⓑ Ⓒ Ⓓ	
18 Ⓐ Ⓑ Ⓒ Ⓓ	23 Ⓐ Ⓑ Ⓒ Ⓓ	
19 Ⓐ Ⓑ Ⓒ Ⓓ	24 Ⓐ Ⓑ Ⓒ Ⓓ	
20 Ⓐ Ⓑ Ⓒ Ⓓ	25 Ⓐ Ⓑ Ⓒ Ⓓ	

PART III

Task A

Identify a method

**Cross out those sentences which do NOT describe a method. Then, in the
remaining sentences, underline the method.**

1   How do you find the right applicant for the job?
    (A) Generally, my first step is to <u>call</u> the candidate and <u>get some information</u> from them.
    (B) ~~The candidate did not have the necessary experience.~~
    (C) ~~She was asking for too much money.~~
    (D) It's best to <u>reject</u> unqualified candidates <u>before interviewing</u> them.

2   What is your secret for running a successful meeting?
    (A) The meeting is always run by the director of the department.
    (B) They are more successful when an agenda is distributed beforehand.
    (C) He tries not to keep them more than an hour and a half.
    (D) For the first time, every single employee was present.

3   How are employee's references checked?
    (A) A background check is done for everyone.
    (B) A sales representative makes a cold call.
    (C) Literature is sent out to the prospective client.
    (D) The office revenue was over $1.5 million.

4   How do you start to develop an advertising campaign?
    (A) After weeks of talks, they refused our terms of agreement.
    (B) Once we know who our audience is, we start to design a message.
    (C) New York advertising costs are some of the highest in the world.
    (D) We do extensive market research.

5   What is included in your background check of an employee?
    (A) All the employees' files are checked for any negative incidents.
    (B) Anyone with unsatisfactory reviews is given a warning.
    (C) The supervisor's evaluations are reviewed.
    (D) They were fired without notice.

Strategy B

Look for questions that ask to identify emotions. Pay attention to questions that begin with *how*. Read the answer choices quickly. Look for words that describe feelings.

How does the man feel?
How will the woman react?

Task B

Identify emotions

Read a line from a conversation. Then cross out the answer choices that are NOT possible.

6   "It's my first time to run the staff meeting."
    How might the woman feel?

    (A) Corrupt.
    (B) Confident.
    (C) Appropriate.
    (D) Apprehensive.

7   "Dr. Lau is retiring after 45 years of service."
    How might the speaker feel toward Dr. Lau?
    (A) Impressed.
    (B) Energetic.
    (C) Envious.
    (D) Incensed.

8   "John will receive his warning letter this afternoon."
    How might John feel?

    (A) Dubious.
    (B) Defensive.
    (C) Defiant.
    (D) Delighted.

9   "The evaluations from the training session were returned with very concrete and helpful comments."
    How have the evaluators felt about the program?

    (A) Critical.
    (B) Evasive.
    (C) Disgusted.
    (D) Avid.

Review

Directions: Listen and choose the best answer to each question.

10   What do they think about Gina?

     (A) She's discreet.
     (B) She can't be trusted.
     (C) She has a good reputation.
     (D) She can keep a secret.

11   How does the woman want to start?

     (A) By cleaning the public spaces.
     (B) By organizing her desk.
     (C) By planning to work weekends.
     (D) By cleaning the shelves.

12   How does the woman deal with her e-mail?

     (A) She reads only the important messages.
     (B) She reads them, then calls the writer.
     (C) She reads them, then deletes them.
     (D) She deletes some without reading them.

13   How does the man feel?

     (A) Obnoxious.
     (B) Frustrated.
     (C) Untroubled.
     (D) Carefree.

Listening Comprehension
Part III
10 (A) (B) (C) (D)
11 (A) (B) (C) (D)
12 (A) (B) (C) (D)
13 (A) (B) (C) (D)

PART IV

Strategy A

Use the questions and answers to focus on specific dates. Look for questions that begin with *when*.

> *When* is the meeting?
> *When* will the new computers arrive?
> *When* is Mr. Lee retiring?

In the answers look for specific date markers which refer to a precise month, day or time.

Specific Date Markers

Months:	in *January, February, March, April,* etc.
Days of the week:	on *Monday, Tuesday, Wednesday, Thursday,* etc.
Time:	at *5:45 a.m*, in *19 weeks*, for *24 minutes*, etc.

Grammar Glossary Adverbs: Date/Time/Sequence Markers (p213)

Task A

Identify specific dates

Cross out the answer choices that do NOT indicate specific dates.

1. (A) Every third Monday of the month.
   (B) On the following Monday at noon.
   (C) At 5:00 p.m. on the day that you choose.
   (D) Any Monday that is convenient for you.

2. (A) It ran from May 23rd through the 29th.
   (B) Fourteen days is the longest trip she has taken.
   (C) It lasted for around two weeks.
   (D) She left for her trip on the fifth of May.

3. (A) He'll start sometime next month.
   (B) He already started working.
   (C) His start date is the Tuesday after next.
   (D) He gave his notice on November 2nd and will begin thirty days after.

4. (A) Your computer will be on your desk first thing in the morning.
   (B) The shipment of new computers was delayed, but they should arrive any day now.
   (C) They guaranteed delivery within twenty-one days from the order date.
   (D) The order arrived yesterday.

5. (A) All evaluations are due in two weeks with no exceptions.
   (B) Evaluations are always given the second Monday of February.
   (C) I received my evaluation three weeks late last year.
   (D) You can turn in the evaluation any time after the first of the month.

6. (A) Mr. Schwartz is celebrating his twentieth year with the company today.
   (B) Jim was promoted on the Monday after we moved into our new offices.
   (C) He began work sometime in May of 1990.
   (D) The office staff is planning a party tomorrow at 5:00 p.m.

Strategy B

Use the questions and answers to identify responsibilities.

Look for questions that begin with *who* to identify the person who is doing something.
Look for questions that begin with *what* to identify the actions the person should do or take.

Who is responsible for hiring?
Who is in charge of the meeting?

What is she responsible for doing?
What are his job responsibilities?

Test note
Often, responsibilities are listed as gerunds (the *-ing* form).

What is he responsible for?
Filing, answering the phones and data entry.

Task B

Identify responsibilities

Listen to two talks. Before each talk begins, read the answer choices quickly. Then choose the best answer.

7   Who must be notified first if an employee is sick?

   (A)   The human resource manager.
   (B)   The supervisor.
   (C)   Giovanni.
   (D)   The company doctor.

8   Who will contact the doctor?

   (A)   The employee.
   (B)   The supervisor.
   (C)   Mark Johnson.
   (D)   The human resource manager.

9   What is each manager expected to do?

   (A)   Discuss plans for the next two years.
   (B)   Report on a region's performance.
   (C)   Outline his or her travel agenda.
   (D)   Organize the next meeting.

10   Who is responsible for the United States?

   (A)   No one.
   (B)   Everyone.
   (C)   The first presenter.
   (D)   The last presenter.

Review

Directions: Listen and choose the best answer to each question.

11   When will employees start to pack their boxes?

   (A)   Wednesday at noon.
   (B)   On Friday.
   (C)   Sometime on Tuesday afternoon.
   (D)   Before Tuesday noon.

12   Who is responsible for organizing the move?

   (A)   Each employee.
   (B)   The announcer.
   (C)   Mark Chow.
   (D)   Suzanne Green.

13   What is Diana Sanchez responsible for?

   (A)   Reading through the package.
   (B)   Driving the group to the meeting.
   (C)   Determining who is in each group.
   (D)   Doing the new employee training.

14   When will the training take place?

   (A)   Next Friday.
   (B)   Today.
   (C)   Over the next three Fridays.
   (D)   Between today and Friday.

Listening Comprehension				
Part IV				
11	Ⓐ	Ⓑ	Ⓒ	Ⓓ
12	Ⓐ	Ⓑ	Ⓒ	Ⓓ
13	Ⓐ	Ⓑ	Ⓒ	Ⓓ
14	Ⓐ	Ⓑ	Ⓒ	Ⓓ

Reading PART V

Strategy A

Look at the sentence to identify the prepositions. Then look what follows the preposition. This is the object. A prepositional phrase is made up of a preposition and an object.

The new employee was given a long list *(of fifteen items)* to be completed *(by the next day)*.

You see two prepositional phrases in the sentence. The prepositions are *of* and *by*. Each has an object: *fifteen items* and *the next day*.

On the TOEIC test, the incomplete part of the sentence may follow a preposition. Check carefully if it is part of a prepositional phrase. If so, the missing word will be a noun – the object of the preposition.

Grammar Glossary **Prepositions: Objects (p218)**

Task A

Identify the objects of prepositions

Mark the prepositional phrase(s) in each of the sentences by placing parentheses around the phrase. Underline the object(s) of the preposition.

1   The entire staff gathered (around the computer) to see the software demonstration.

2   She had only three days remaining of her vacation time, so she received no pay for the other ten days of her trip.

3   The supervisor, after serious thought, denied his employee's request for a leave of absence.

4   When the company won the contract with the government, it had to begin a policy requiring all employees with access to the building to wear identification badges.

5   Everyone in the office gave some money to purchase a farewell gift for Ms. Woo.

6   The memo was lost in a pile of papers that ended up on the secretary's desk.

Strategy B

Read the answer choices quickly to find the correct word. If you see similar prefixes or suffixes, be careful to choose the word with the correct meaning.

> The director of personnel .... the resumes before the candidates came for an interview.
>   (A) preselected
>   (B) preferred
>   (C) predicted
>   (D) previewed

You can quickly see that the common prefix is *pre-*, meaning *before*. Read the second part of each word carefully to work out the answer.

D, *previewed* is correct. The second part of the word *viewed* meaning *looked at*, so the director *looked at* the resumes *before* the candidates came for an interview.

Grammar Glossary **Prefixes and Suffixes (p217)**

Task B

Identify the correct word

Check the word which has the same meaning as the underlined word.
Then enter the common prefix or suffix.

7   She <u>looked through</u> the pile of applications.
     (A) recalled
     (B) reviewed ✓
     (C) reinforced
     (D) reassessed

     Common prefix or suffix: ...*re-*...

8   The manager called the <u>referee</u> to inquire about the applicant.
     (A) reference
     (B) residence
     (C) precedence
     (D) inference

     Common prefix or suffix: ....

9   The board meeting was <u>delayed</u> due to members being out of the country.
     (A) postulated
     (B) posterior
     (C) postmarked
     (D) postponed

     Common prefix or suffix: ....

10   The audience thought the Korean dancers were <u>marvellous.</u>
     (A) terrific
     (B) realistic
     (C) authentic
     (D) ethnic

     Common prefix or suffix: ....

11   The award <u>consisted of</u> a trip to the Bahamas and a check for $5,000.
     (A) included
     (B) insisted
     (C) incorporated
     (D) influenced

     Common prefix or suffix: ....

Review

Directions: Choose the one word that best completes the sentence.

12 With all the clutter, the customer didn't have a very favorable .... of the office.
(A) revision
(B) provision
(C) impression
(D) vision

13 All workers have the right to review the terms of their ....
(A) employ
(B) employment
(C) employee
(D) employed

14 She met with the .... firm as soon as she finished her degree.
(A) recruitment
(B) recruits
(C) recruited
(D) recruit

15 They made a mistake in not considering the .... of leasing the office furniture.
(A) option
(B) operating
(C) opinion
(D) opposition

16 The year was so .... for the company that every employee received an additional 10% bonus.
(A) professional
(B) prolific
(C) proactive
(D) profitable

Reading				
Part V				
12	Ⓐ	Ⓑ	Ⓒ	Ⓓ
13	Ⓐ	Ⓑ	Ⓒ	Ⓓ
14	Ⓐ	Ⓑ	Ⓒ	Ⓓ
15	Ⓐ	Ⓑ	Ⓒ	Ⓓ
16	Ⓐ	Ⓑ	Ⓒ	Ⓓ

PART VI

Read the sentence quickly to identify the time frame in which it is taking place. Make sure that all the verbs indicate the correct time frame for the context of the sentence.

> The licensee, who *had experienced* financial difficulties for years, finally *closed* his business and *liquidated* his merchandise.

Looking at the sentence quickly shows three different verbs: *had experienced*, in the past perfect tense, and *closed* and *liquidated*, in the past simple.

By identifying the past perfect, you know that the rest of the sentence will probably indicate a past time.

Grammar Glossary **Verb Tenses** (p220)

Task A

Identify the verb tenses

Underline the verbs in the sentence and write their tenses.

1   The temporary receptionist's work <u>has been</u> so impressive that the director <u>is offering</u> him a full-time job today!
    present perfect, present continuous
    ....

2   Everyone in the office knew about the division's personnel problems, but no one wanted to tell the president.
    ....

3   The number of employees who are asking for flexible schedules is on the increase.
    ....

4   He didn't want to be disturbed, so he asked his assistant to redirect all calls during his morning meeting.
    ....

5   Due to the restructuring, this office will be closed and all the employees will relocate to the head office or work out of their homes.
    ....

Strategy B

Look out for incorrect pronouns. On the TOEIC test, an incorrect form of the pronoun is often used for the noun it refers to.

> His file should have been on the interviewer's desk, but instead they was eventually found with the training manuals.

His file is the subject of the sentence. This object is singular and refers to a man's file. Later in the sentence, the pronoun *they* is used to refer back to the subject. The correct pronoun in this case is *it* and not *they*. It also agrees with the verb form used *was*.

Grammar Glossary Pronouns (p218)

Task B

Identify the correct form of the pronoun

Underline the correct pronouns.

6 Even though Maria has several years of marketing experience, <u>it</u> / they was with a completely different industry and we don't feel that <u>it</u> / they will help we / <u>us</u>.

7 They / Their offices will be closed for the holiday so you should call he / him back on Tuesday morning.

8 All of he / his preparation served his / him well when he / him began the training program.

9 The fax machine will automatically redial she / her number if it / her is busy the first try.

10 The managers want to change it / their company's phone system so that it / their customers don't have to listen to a lengthy recording.

11 Because it / their employees work such long hours, the executive management team have decided to construct a gym in the basement of its / their facilities which everyone can use.

12 In order to boost its / they profits, Ikon has begun Spanish language classes for executives.

13 As soon as she / her reached she / her five year mark, she / her turned in she / her letter of resignation.

14 Ms. Lu will take you / your through we / our Start Program to begin the training.

15 It was he / his responsibility to confirm they / their plans and that everything would be ready.

Review

Directions: Identify the one underlined word or phrase that should be corrected or rewritten.

16   In a <u>surprising trend</u>, the newspaper <u>noting</u> that more minority employees <u>were being</u>
               A   B   C
    promoted than <u>ever before</u>.
                            D

17   The government <u>is expected</u> to make <u>their</u> decision on the <u>minimum</u> wage <u>policy</u> in the next few days.
                         A   B   C   D

18   <u>Contract negotiations</u> with the labor union <u>become</u> very heated <u>as the deadline</u> drew <u>nearer</u>.
              A   B   C   D

19   <u>In part</u>, she <u>was attracted</u> to the company because of <u>his</u> casual <u>dress policy</u>.
        A   B   C   D

20   <u>Once</u> she finishes <u>her</u> probationary period, <u>it would</u> be very difficult to fire <u>her</u>.
       A   B   C   D

21   The atmosphere <u>in the office</u> changed dramatically <u>after</u> the manager <u>is</u> moved to a <u>satellite office</u>.
                     A   B   C   D

22   The staff looked to <u>he</u> for <u>guidance</u> as he <u>had been running</u> the office <u>for such a long time</u>.
                       A   B   C   D

23   The phone <u>has been</u> <u>out of order</u> since <u>him</u> came <u>in</u> at 7:00 a.m.
                 A   B   C   D

24   <u>Their</u> threw <u>her</u> a party <u>to thank</u> her for many years <u>of service</u> and dedication.
       A   B   C   D

25   The last person <u>in the office</u> <u>must have make sure</u> to lock <u>all the doors</u> and <u>turn off</u> the computers.
                    A   B   C   D

Reading

Part VI				
16	Ⓐ	Ⓑ	Ⓒ	Ⓓ
17	Ⓐ	Ⓑ	Ⓒ	Ⓓ
18	Ⓐ	Ⓑ	Ⓒ	Ⓓ
19	Ⓐ	Ⓑ	Ⓒ	Ⓓ
20	Ⓐ	Ⓑ	Ⓒ	Ⓓ
21	Ⓐ	Ⓑ	Ⓒ	Ⓓ
22	Ⓐ	Ⓑ	Ⓒ	Ⓓ
23	Ⓐ	Ⓑ	Ⓒ	Ⓓ
24	Ⓐ	Ⓑ	Ⓒ	Ⓓ
25	Ⓐ	Ⓑ	Ⓒ	Ⓓ

PART VII

Where does Mr. Johns suggest holding the meeting?
- (A) In Gaylor St.
- (B) In Spain
- (C) At his office
- (D) At the Los Angeles office

Ms. Joanne Swift
Director of Human Resources
Convac Financial Services
1122 Gaylor St.
Los Angeles, CA 92710

Dear Ms. Swift:

I received your message yesterday concerning an interview time. I am very interested in meeting with you. Unfortunately, I will be in Spain on a business trip from June 30 through July 6. Would it be possible to meet at your office in Los Angeles sometime during the week of July 10?

Please contact me at your earliest convenience.

Sincerely,

Jay Johns

From the question, you know to look for a location. Reading the letter quickly, you see a number of places: *Gaylor St., Los Angeles* and *Spain*. Mr. Johns wrote the letter to Ms. Swift, asking specifically for an interview in Ms. Swift's Los Angeles office. The correct answer is (D).

Task A

Identify a location

Choose the answer choice that does NOT have an example of the underlined word.

1   Ms. Jones has lived in six different <u>countries</u>.
    (A) Austria has a reputation for its conservative population.
    (B) The director has only positive things to say about London.
    (C) The winters are difficult in Canada.
    (D) They closed the office in Hong Kong.

2   Our office has changed <u>streets</u>.
    (A) On the second floor of 532 Muenster
    (B) Parallel to 9 de Julio Boulevard
    (C) In Exeter
    (D) At the corner of Pine and Sarasota

3   The firm is closed for all <u>major holidays</u>.
    (A) New Year's Day is celebrated at different times by different cultures.
    (B) In some countries, the first of May, May Day, honors workers.
    (C) Christmas, Ramadan, and Passover are all marked by religious ceremonies.
    (D) The office is open only from Monday to Friday.

4   The manager will relocate to our <u>city</u> for her new job.
    (A) She will have to move to Geneva.
    (B) California is experiencing a real growth in population.
    (C) Paris is a perfect place for her and her family.
    (D) Four employees have moved to Jakarta over the last year.

Strategy B

Read the answer choices and passage quickly to look for explanations. Questions that begin with *why* often ask for an explanation.

Why are they having a meeting on Friday?
       (A) To finish the paperwork
       (B) To accommodate people who can't meet today
       (C) To sign up outside of her office
       (D) To go over the old health plan

To...	**WILLIS,Barry**
From...	**BENNET,JANE**
Subject:	**Announcement**

There will be a meeting of all full-time staff this afternoon at 3:30 in the small conference room. The purpose of the meeting is to review the new health plan and complete all the necessary paperwork. If you are unable to make the meeting today, there will be another meeting on Friday at 10:00. Sign up for the day you will be attending on the sheets outside of my office.

(B) is the correct answer. The question asks for an explanation for the Friday meeting. Reading the answer choices quickly, you see that all of them begin with *to*. All of them may give an explanation, but do they all answer the question? (A) answers the question, but incorrectly and not according to the announcement. (C) answers another question, *"What should the staff do?"* and is therefore incorrect. (D) indicates the old health plan and not the new health plan as stated in the announcement. The correct answer, (B), explains why a second meeting will be held on Friday.

Task B

Identify an explanation

Match the explanations (A–F) with the questions (5–10).

5   Why is she leaving her job? ....

6   Why are they revising the office safety procedures? ....

7   Why do they hire so many new employees? ....

8   Why will he wait until next week to hold the meeting? ....

9   Why has she been working so much overtime? ....

10 Why were they removed from the Board of Directors? ....

(A)   To bring them up to national standards.

(B)   There are too many people on vacation this week.

(C)   She was offered a job in Europe where her family lives.

(D)   She is going on vacation for three weeks and has a lot of work to finish before then.

(E)   The others didn't feel that they were doing an adequate job.

(F)   To make sure that they aren't short-staffed during the holidays.

Review

Directions: Read the letter and choose the one best answer (A), (B), (C) or (D) to each question.

Questions 11–14 refer to the following letter.

Valentina Saguier
Office Manager
270 Siena
Asuncion, Paraguay

Dear Ms. Saguier:

Thank you for your recent payment for your Villarica account.

Unfortunately, we still have not received payment for your store branch 11. The Encarnacion account has been late for the last 4 months. If we do not receive payment within 15 days, we will be forced to cancel this account.

We understand that you are expanding and now have stores throughout the country, with your main office located in Miami. However, we cannot overlook the amount of money that is due and the manner in which payments are made.

Please contact us immediately or send the outstanding payment to our Accounting Department here in Boston.

Sincerely,

Federico Marquez

11 Why did Mr. Marquez write the letter?
(A) To warn of pending action.
(B) To thank Ms. Saguier for the payment.
(C) To cancel an account in Villarica.
(D) To congratulate Ms. Saguier on her expansion.

12 Where is store branch 11?
(A) In the United States.
(B) In Boston.
(C) In Encarnacion.
(D) In Asuncion.

13 Why does he think that it is difficult for Ms. Saguier to make the payments?
(A) Many of the stores are closing.
(B) They have stores in many different locations.
(C) She doesn't understand the business.
(D) She lives in Miami.

14 Where is Federico Marquez located?
(A) In Miami.
(B) In Encarnacion.
(C) In the branch in Asuncion.
(D) At an office in Boston.

Reading			
Part VII			
11	Ⓐ Ⓑ © Ⓓ		
12	Ⓐ Ⓑ © Ⓓ		
13	Ⓐ Ⓑ © Ⓓ		
14	Ⓐ Ⓑ © Ⓓ		

Listening comprehension PART I

Strategy A

Use the pictures to identify an action. Ask yourself *who* the person is, *what* they are doing, *where* they are doing it.

Who?   The waiter *is assisting* the diners.
What?   The waiter *is waiting* to take their order.
Where? The waiter *is standing* between the diners.

Who?   The chef *is preparing* some food.
What?   The chef *is using* a knife to slice the food.
Where? The chef *is working* in the kitchen.

Task A

Identify an action

Write the appropriate verb from the list below to complete the sentence.

buying   checking   reserving   ~~confirming~~   ordering

1   The host is *confirming* the reservations for a party of twelve.

2   The businessman is .... appetizers for everyone.

3   The couple are .... tickets to the movies.

4   The usher is .... the date on the theater ticket.

5   The secretary is .... a table for eight.

Strategy B

Be aware of similar sounds. The TOEIC® test often uses similar sounding words to confuse you. Note the similar sounding words in these examples.

(A) They're sitting in a row.
(B) They're looking very low.
(C) They're walking by a rink.
(D) They're moving their seats.

The correct answer is (A).

(A) She's counting trinkets.
(B) She's playing cricket.
(C) She's sailing in a race.
(D) She's selling a ticket.

The correct answer is (D).

Task B

Identify the similar sounding words

Listen to the pairs of sentences. Mark *1* beside the word you hear in the first sentence and *2* beside the word you hear in the second sentence.

6   seating ....
    sitting ....

7   tip ....
    trip ....

8   glass ....
    grass ....

9   line ....
    lime ....

10 cash ....
    catch ....

Review 📼

Directions: Listen to the statements and choose the one that best describes what you see in the picture.

11

12

13

14

Listening Comprehension

Part I				
11	Ⓐ	Ⓑ	Ⓒ	Ⓓ
12	Ⓐ	Ⓑ	Ⓒ	Ⓓ
13	Ⓐ	Ⓑ	Ⓒ	Ⓓ
14	Ⓐ	Ⓑ	Ⓒ	Ⓓ

PART II

Task A

Identify the person or occupation

Cross out the answer choices that are NOT possible.

1   Who is talking to the group at the door?

   (A)   To be seated for dinner.
   (B)   The head waiter.
   (C)   It must be the hostess.

2   Who is your favorite musician?

   (A)   Classical is my favorite.
   (B)   It's Michael Jackson.
   (C)   I have several favorites.

3   Who organized the banquet?

   (A)   I believe it was Mark.
   (B)   The bank called earlier today.
   (C)   Several people were involved.

4   Who should I talk to about a formal reception?

   (A)   There are professional planners who can help.
   (B)   It should be an informal event.
   (C)   Jose's assistant did a good job last year.

5   Who is going to pick up the lunch bill today?

   (A)   It's quite inexpensive.
   (B)   I did yesterday!
   (C)   Why don't we split it?

6   Who is the painter of this picture?

   (A)   The artist that lives on the beach.
   (B)   In the mid-1800s.
   (C)   Isn't that a Picasso?

7   Who is in charge of ticket sales?

   (A)   Last year it was the marketing director.
   (B)   You can still buy tickets.
   (C)   The elderly man with the black suit.

8   Who recommended this restaurant?

   (A)   I had the fish special.
   (B)   It sure wasn't me!
   (C)   I wish I could take credit.

9   Who would like an appetizer?

   (A)   I would love something sweet before we leave.
   (B)   Is anyone else getting one?
   (C)   Andrea wants the stuffed mushrooms.

10   To whom do I give my coat check?

   (A)   I'll take it.
   (B)   The check is for $4.
   (C)   The man in the burgundy vest.

Real Spoken English
Who do I give my coat check to? is probably heard more often than the grammatically correct *To whom do I give my coat check?*

Strategy B

Listen for questions that ask about the relationship between people.

How do they know each other?
What is the relationship between the man and the woman?
Who is the woman at the party?
To whom is the man speaking?

Task B

Identify relationships

Read the two lines of the conversation. Then choose the most likely relationship between the speakers.

11   **A:** Why did you choose this restaurant?
      B: It's large enough for a meeting of all the new managers.

     (A) Two employees.
     (B) The chef and a busboy.
     (C) An athlete and coach.

12   **A:** Who was the artist working with before coming here?
      B: She was with that avant-garde group in Moscow, Tseliy.

     (A) A journalist and the gallery owner.
     (B) A gallery owner and the artist.
     (C) An employer and a Russian collector.

13   **A:** I want to speak with your boss right now. Who is your boss?
      B: Then you can talk with me, I'm the boss.

     (A) The president and the CEO.
     (B) A supervisor and her employee.
     (C) An angry customer and a woman at the cash register.

14   **A:** Where can I buy tickets?
      B: The woman in the green dress can help you.

     (A) A director and an actor.
     (B) An usher and a theater patron.
     (C) A sales clerk and a manager.

15   **A:** Have you heard the speaker before?
      B: I've heard him several times at marketing seminars, and each time he was excellent.

     (A) An actor and a fan.
     (B) Two advertising managers.
     (C) The speaker and his manager.

Review

Directions: Listen and choose the best response to each question.

Listening Comprehension

Part II			
16	Ⓐ	Ⓑ	Ⓒ
17	Ⓐ	Ⓑ	Ⓒ
18	Ⓐ	Ⓑ	Ⓒ
19	Ⓐ	Ⓑ	Ⓒ
20	Ⓐ	Ⓑ	Ⓒ
21	Ⓐ	Ⓑ	Ⓒ
22	Ⓐ	Ⓑ	Ⓒ
23	Ⓐ	Ⓑ	Ⓒ
24	Ⓐ	Ⓑ	Ⓒ
25	Ⓐ	Ⓑ	Ⓒ

PART III

Strategy A

Use the questions and answers to identify the topic of conversation. Look for questions that begin with what. Then try to anticipate what the conversation will be about from the question and from each option.

If you read a question *What is the woman trying to do?* you need to understand the main idea.

If you read the answer choices
    (A) Buy a new coat.   (C) Move to a sunny place.
    (B) Try to stay warm.   (D) Go out on a boat.
you could anticipate that the topic of conversation may be about the cold weather or a vacation.

Test note
Questions about the topic of conversation are very common on the TOEIC test. Generally, you don't need to focus on details for these types of questions.

Task A

Identify the topic of conversation

Match the parts of a conversation to the appropriate answer choices.

1   (A) Susan did not like the meal.
    (B) Susan has to get back to work.
    (C) They have been waiting for a while.
    (D) They are waiting for their meals.

    How much longer will we have to wait? ...*C*.....
    At least they brought us bread and drinks. ...*D*.......
    I'll never go back to that place. ...*A*......
    I'm not sure if I have time for dessert. ...*B*......

2   (A) Verify the type of payment.
    (B) Book someone to prepare the food.
    (C) Confirm a place to have the party.
    (D) Find a music group.

    Marc has a list of caterers from the past years. ....

    Carol always has good suggestions for bands. ....

    I haven't reserved the room yet for our reception. ....

    He's not sure if they accept personal checks. ....

3   (A) The party will be moved to a larger room.
    (B) The woman may sit with a relative.
    (C) The guests won't know where to sit.
    (D) Guests may have to wait to hear the main attraction.

    The name cards haven't been placed on the tables yet. ....
    They aren't sure of the room yet because there are more people than expected. ....
    If the keynote speaker arrives on time, she will speak first. ....
    If my cousin doesn't come, I'd love to sit with you. ....

4   (A) This means the show is about to begin.
    (B) The play will have three parts.
    (C) After the play, the audience will have an opportunity to discuss it.
    (D) The director will not allow any interruptions.

    No latecomers are seated until the intermission. ....
    There are two, fifteen-minute breaks. ....
    When the lights blink, you will have five minutes to find your seats. ....
    A short talk will follow the performance. ....

5   (A) The event is casual.
    (B) Transportation is being provided for everyone.
    (C) Employees don't need to purchase tickets.
    (D) The company sponsors an annual event.

    The bus will be at the front door at 5:00 p.m. promptly. ....
    Don't worry about what you wear. ....
    Is it a problem if she didn't buy a ticket? ....
    We all went to the game together last year for the first time. ....

Strategy B

Use the questions and answer choices to limit where the action is taking place.
Pay attention to questions that begin with *where*. Cross out those answer choices that do NOT answer the question *where*.

Where is the speaker?

(A) ~~She's talking to the professor.~~   (C) ~~She is the recipient of the award.~~
(B) She's sitting at the head table.   (D) She was at the hotel.

The correct answer is (B). You can immediately eliminate (A) which answers *What is she doing*? and (C) which answers *Who is the speaker*? because they don't answer the question *Where … ?*. (B) and (D) answer the question *Where … ?*, but (D) is in the past tense and the question is in the present tense. Therefore, you know the answer is (B).

Task B

Identify the location of an action

Read a line from a conversation. Identify where the conversation most likely takes place. Then underline the prepositions.

6   I'm not feeling well, so I'll meet you at our seats after intermission.
Where is the conversation taking place?

(A) At the doctor's office.
(B) In the lobby of a hotel.
(C) Outside the theater.
(D) In the dressing room.

7   My sister-in-law, who loves art, is very impressed with his brush work and colours.
Where are they?

(A) At a restaurant.
(B) At a business seminar.
(C) At a museum exhibit.
(D) At a gift store.

8   The board room, where we'll meet after lunch, is just downstairs.
Where is the speaker?

(A) At a café eating lunch.
(B) At the butcher's.
(C) In the board room.
(D) In the office.

9   I came to Hawaii after having visited some smaller Pacific islands first.
Where is the speaker?

(A) In Hawaii.
(B) Over the ocean.
(C) In Australia.
(D) On a little island in the Pacific.

Review

Directions: Listen and choose the best answer to each question.

10   What will the woman do?

(A) Go to her favorite restaurant.
(B) Call a friend who lives in the city.
(C) Ask someone at the hotel.
(D) Look in a book.

11   Where did they see the show?

(A) At the boat club.
(B) At the beach.
(C) On a boat.
(D) At a dance club.

12   What does the man imply about art?

(A) It should be inspirational.
(B) It is undervalued.
(C) It is easy to look at.
(D) It is expensive.

13   Where is the conversation taking place?

(A) At a furniture store.
(B) At a museum.
(C) At a theater.
(D) In the lobby.

Listening Comprehension
Part III
10 (A) (B) (C) (D)
11 (A) (B) (C) (D)
12 (A) (B) (C) (D)
13 (A) (B) (C) (D)

PART IV

Use the questions and answers to focus on the topic of the talks. Look for questions that begin with *what*.

> *What* are the people talking about?
> *What* is the speaker referring to?
> *What* is the theme of the talk?

Listen carefully to the first sentence for clues to the main topic. As you listen to the talk, try to focus on the main idea.

Task A 📼

Identify the main topic of the conversation

Listen to three talks. Before each talk begins, read the answer choices quickly. Then choose the best answer choice.

Test note
The conversations in this part of the TOEIC test may contain many distracting details, such as times or dates. From the question, however, you should be able to determine the relevance of such details in advance. Don't waste time focusing on information that you don't need.

1   What is the purpose of the dinner?

(A) To escape the weather.
(B) To give awards to all employees.
(C) To present five honors.
(D) To introduce all the new employees.

2   What will happen next?

(A) Mrs. Nakashima will receive an award.
(B) The guests will take a vote.
(C) The employees will be more successful.
(D) Mrs. Nakashima will announce a winner.

3   What is the purpose of the advertisement?

(A) To present a new menu.
(B) To announce a reopening.
(C) To tell about a conference center.
(D) To provide topics of conversation.

4   What does the speaker recommend?

(A) Visiting the restaurant.
(B) Eating breakfast early.
(C) Calling for reservations.
(D) Asking for a booth.

5   What is the speaker referring to?

(A) Shorter hours at the museum.
(B) Increase in entrance fees.
(C) A new exhibition.
(D) A computerized reservation system.

6   What is the museum expecting?

(A) Lots of visitors.
(B) Decreased number of tour groups.
(C) Celebrity visitors.
(D) Expensive tickets.

Strategy B

Use the questions and answers to focus on the order of events. Look for questions that begin with *when* and *what*. Pay attention to words about sequence such as *first*, *next*, and *finally*.

When will they take the next step?
What will happen next?
In what order will they finish?

Grammar Glossary Adverbs: Sequence Markers (p213)

Task B

Identify the steps in a process

Put the events in order from 1–3.

7 Then you must confirm all reservations. ....
First, make sure that all the tables are ready. ....
When the guests arrive, show them to their tables. ....

8 Any outstanding business will be taken care of first. ....
Lastly, we need to plan for the upcoming year. ....
After that, our vice president will speak. ....

9 Meet me at 7:30 outside the restaurant. ....
Call to make reservations for a party of six. ....
Let's choose a restaurant first. ....

10 We suggest that you listen to the cassette before entering the exhibit. ....
Make sure you plan to come back to see our exhibit next month. ....
After you've gone through each room, return to your favorite paintings. ....

Review 📼

Directions: Listen and choose the best answer to each question.

11 What is the purpose of the announcement?
   (A) To announce the winner.
   (B) To explain what will happen during the break.
   (C) To sell tickets for the raffle.
   (D) To plan a Mediterranean trip.

12 What will happen after the raffle?
   (A) The concert will continue.
   (B) Guests may get something to eat.
   (C) There will be an intermission.
   (D) The patrons will go home.

13 What is the speaker explaining?
   (A) How antiques are found.
   (B) The types of hotel rooms available.
   (C) How the auction will work.
   (D) Where guests should buy food.

14 What should visitors do before the auction?
   (A) Examine the antiques to be sold.
   (B) Reserve a room at the hotel.
   (C) Return their paddles to the ballroom.
   (D) Place a bid with the auctioneer.

Listening Comprehension

Part IV				
11	Ⓐ	Ⓑ	Ⓒ	Ⓓ
12	Ⓐ	Ⓑ	Ⓒ	Ⓓ
13	Ⓐ	Ⓑ	Ⓒ	Ⓓ
14	Ⓐ	Ⓑ	Ⓒ	Ⓓ

Reading PART V

Strategy A

You can often identify a profession or occupation by the ending of the noun.
Many professions and occupations end in *-er* , *-or* or *-ist*.

The .... each have eight tables tonight.
(A)   waiting
(B)   waiters
(C)   waits
(D)   waited

Each of the answer choices is from the same word family. (B) is the correct
answer as it ends in *-ers*, which indicates an occupation *-er* and the plural *-s*.
(A) is a gerund, (C) is the simple verb form, and (D) is the past tense of the verb.

> **Grammar Glossary Nouns: Suffixes (p216)**

Task A

Identify the occupation

**Write the part of speech (*noun, verb, adverb, adjective, past participle* or *gerund*) for each answer choice.
Mark O by the form which indicates an occupation. Then choose the word that best completes the sentence.**

1   The ...*sculptor*... is best known for his large stone
    figures.
    (A)   sculpture ...*noun*......
    (B)   sculpt ....*verb*......
    (C)   sculptor *noun (O)*...
    (D)   sculpted ...*past participle*...

2   We waited after the show to congratulate him on
    his .... of the play.
    (A)   director ....
    (B)   directly ....
    (C)   direction ....
    (D)   directed ....

3   I gave the .... our tickets and then he
    disappeared!
    (A)   ushered ....
    (B)   ushering ....
    (C)   ushers ....
    (D)   usher ....

4   The city is honored to have such prominent
    .... displayed in the municipal building.
    (A)   artist ....
    (B)   art ....
    (C)   artfully ....
    (D)   artistic ....

5   When the previous .... retired, she
    bought the restaurant.
    (A)   owned ....
    (B)   owners ....
    (C)   owns ....
    (D)   owning ....

6   He is well-known for being a gracious and
    generous ....
    (A)   hosting ....
    (B)   hostess ....
    (C)   host ....
    (D)   hosted ....

Strategy B

Read the sentence quickly to see what form of the pronoun is needed. Check to see if the pronoun refers to a singular or plural subject.

<u>The business men</u> all looked surprised when the waiter offered *them* a free drink with *their* meal.

By identifying the subject as being plural, you know that the pronouns should be in the third person plural form.

Grammar Glossary **Nouns: Singular/Plural (p216)   Pronouns (p219)**

Task B

Identify the correct pronoun

Complete the sentence with the correct form of a pronoun.

7   The women prefer to have ......*their*........ lunch at noon.

 That woman has ......*her*........ lunch here everyday.

8   The manager and .... wife both attended the reception.

 The couple wanted .... party to be a success.

9   My feet are tired. I'll stop dancing and give .... a rest.

 My foot hurts. I think I'll put ice on ....

10   Isn't that the child who played "Jack" in that movie? ....'s a fantastic actor.

 The children are too young to watch that movie, so we'll have to ask .... grandparents to babysit.

11   I'm looking for the knives? Have you seen .... ?

 I've dropped my knife. Could you pick .... up for me please?

Review

Directions: Choose the one word that best completes the sentence.

12 In order to be a successful .... for the city, the candidate must have key contacts in all areas of business.

    (A) fundraising
    (B) fundraise
    (C) fundraiser
    (D) fundraisers

13 All of .... donations will be sent to help needy children.

    (A) ours
    (B) it
    (C) your
    (D) you

14 He made a .... for six people.

    (A) reserve
    (B) reservation
    (C) reserving
    (D) reserved

15 As the .... of the newly restored theater, she took on the task of making the public aware of the changes.

    (A) managing
    (B) managed
    (C) management
    (D) manager

16 Since the managing director was not able to attend the awards dinner, the award was given to .... in absentia.

    (A) she
    (B) hers
    (C) his
    (D) her

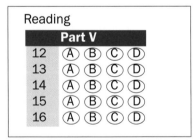

PART VI

Grammar Glossary Comparatives and Superlatives (p214)

Task A

Identify the correct comparative or superlative form

Underline the correct form of the adjective.

1 The Egyptian antiquity exhibit was the *larger / largest* of its kind in more than fifty years.

2 The restaurant has prided itself on its innovative menu since its *earliest / earlier* days.

3 The opening performance of the opera received *more / most* positive comments than the debut of the city orchestra.

4 Our new client is very selective, so we must pick between the *better / best* of the two recommendations.

5 *The most rewarding / The more rewarding* comment she ever gave me was about my performance in Macbeth.

Strategy B

Look out for incorrect conjunctions. Pay attention when a conjunction is one of the underlined choices.

The director <u>insisted on</u> <u>paying</u> not only <u>for</u> dinner <u>and</u> also for the show
afterwards.   A   B   C   D

And is a conjunction, but in this case *not only* gives you a clue about the conjunction that should follow. The fourth answer (D) is incorrect. It should be the conjunction *but*.

Grammar Glossary Conjunctions (p215) >

Task B

Identify the correct conjunction

Determine which conjunction should be used and where it should be inserted in the sentence.

6   We ordered dessert at the same time as we ordered our main dish ^ we didn't have very much time. (*so, because*)
    because

7   The waiter forgot our wine, he offered us a complimentary dinner. (*or, so*)

8   The regional director called his wife he was leaving the office for the reception. (*as, so*)

9   If you haven't received your invitation by the end of next week, you want to attend the event, please call our offices. (*because, and*)

10 They accept credit cards, checks, cash for any room service orders. (*but, and*)

11 We can book a tour of the sights in the city, we need to know two days in advance. (*because, but*)

12 Our company was the recipient of tremendous community support after the flood in 2002, we want to help those devastated by this year's storm. (*but, so*)

13 He was expected to attend the wedding of the director's daughter represent the division. (*and, that*)

14 We should meet at 6:30 we aren't late for the festivities. (*because, so that*)

15 Her boss gave her tickets to the opera all the overtime she has worked lately. (*since, because of*)

76   CHAPTER 2, PART VI

Review

Directions: Identify the one underlined word or phrase that should be corrected or rewritten.

16 The artist, although he tried his better, was unable to play his role persuasively.
                   A   B   C   D

17 He wasn't sure what he should wear to the wedding, because he wore a conservative gray suit.
                          A   B   C   D

18 She called the café and left a message that she shouldn't be most than 30 minutes late.
                            A   B   C   D

19 *The Times'* critic called the musician one of the brighter stars to appear in the last year.
          A   B   C   D

20 We can divide the bill but no one will have to pay too much.
           A   B   C   D

21 The gift store has a beautiful selection of the photographer's work which is said to be one of
                                                 A   B   C

the most extensively in the country.
          D

22 Would you like to have your coffee with dessert so after dessert?
                  A   B   C   D

23 They have a special luncheon menu that includes more reasonable priced food.
                    A   B   C   D

24 All beverages and appetizers are compliment due to the unexpected delay of the speaker.
                     A   B   C   D

25 But there were so many people in the line, the usher never even collected my ticket.
       A   B   C   D

Reading

Part VI				
16	Ⓐ	Ⓑ	Ⓒ	Ⓓ
17	Ⓐ	Ⓑ	Ⓒ	Ⓓ
18	Ⓐ	Ⓑ	Ⓒ	Ⓓ
19	Ⓐ	Ⓑ	Ⓒ	Ⓓ
20	Ⓐ	Ⓑ	Ⓒ	Ⓓ
21	Ⓐ	Ⓑ	Ⓒ	Ⓓ
22	Ⓐ	Ⓑ	Ⓒ	Ⓓ
23	Ⓐ	Ⓑ	Ⓒ	Ⓓ
24	Ⓐ	Ⓑ	Ⓒ	Ⓓ
25	Ⓐ	Ⓑ	Ⓒ	Ⓓ

PART VII

Use the questions and answers to focus on the main topic of the passage. Read the questions and answer choices before you read the passage. Then eliminate the answer choices that are irrelevant to the main topic of discussion.

What is the main topic of the notice?
(A)   The renovation of the theater
(B)   The illustrations in the lobby
(C)   The format of the evening
(D)   The actors in the play

Notice

Please note that there will be no intermission for tonight's performance. The running time of the play is one hour and forty-five minutes. We ask all patrons to refrain from leaving their seats until the end of the show. After the show, there will be a discussion open to the public, led by our illustrious cast. Please join us.

The question above asks you for the main topic. By reading the question and answer choices first, you know what to scan for. You can narrow the possible answer choices by discarding any choices that do not contain relevant information.

Scan the notice to see which answer choices you can eliminate. (A) can be eliminated as a theater renovation is not mentioned. (B) contains the word illustrations, which is similar to illustrious in the last sentence. However, neither word relates to the topic of the notice. A synonym for actors in answer choice (D) is cast; however, this isn't the main idea of the notice. Therefore, (C), the format, or what will happen that evening, is the correct answer.

Task A

Identify the topic

Cross out the answer choices that are NOT related to the main underlined topic.

1   Crossroads Café announced its <u>grand opening</u>.
   - (A)   Location
   - (B)   Hours
   - (C)   Menu
   - (D)   City sights

2   The <u>schedule of events</u> was printed for the banquet.
   - (A)   The name of the chef
   - (B)   The key speaker
   - (C)   Dinner
   - (D)   Awards presentation

3   The <u>chamber concert</u> is an overwhelming success.
   - (A)   The program that they played
   - (B)   The new room that was inaugurated
   - (C)   The musicians
   - (D)   A famous person in the audience

4   Visit these <u>popular, new places</u> in Denver.
   - (A)   A new mayor
   - (B)   The best night clubs
   - (C)   Benefits of tanning salons
   - (D)   World-class restaurants

Strategy B

Read the questions, answer choices and passage quickly to identify the people involved. Make sure that you look for the person who is asked about in the question.

To whom is the notice directed?
(A)   The management
(B)   The owners
(C)   The laundry service
(D)   The waiters

Please note that at the end of your shift, you must do the following:
- fill all condiment trays
- stock the utensil trays
- put all dirty linens in the laundry service basket
- divide tips between bartenders and busboys
- check to confirm your next shift

If the following steps are followed, our operations will be much smoother.

Thank you,
The Management

(D) is the correct answer. You know from the question that you need to identify the audience. Two of the answer choices are mentioned in the notice, management and laundry service. The management wrote the notice, so you can eliminate answer choice (A). The laundry service is involved in one part of the notice, but is not the audience, so answer choice (C) can be eliminated. You are left with two choices: (B) and (D). It is unlikely that management would tell owners what to do, or that owners would be responsible for the tasks that are listed, so (B) is not the correct response. Waiters are not mentioned; however if you understand *condiments*, *utensils*, *tips*, *bartenders* or *busboys*, you should be able to identify that the notice refers to a restaurant and that the audience is (D).

Task B

Identify the people

Cross out the person or people in each group who do NOT fit with the majority.
Then write where the remaining people most probably work.

5   manager, cook, ~~reservation clerk~~, busboy, ~~inspector~~, waiter, ~~concierge~~, hostess
They work at a ....*restaurant*............ .

6   director, flight attendant, usher, guide, cast, actors, ticket taker, conductor, civil engineer,
They work at a ....

7   maitre d', docent, ticket taker, server, guide, exhibitor, artist-in-residence, police
They work at a ....

8   disc jockey, program manager, director, usher, sound engineer, newscaster, tour guide
They work at a ....

9   caterer, sound engineer, delivery service, chef, dish washer, attendant, owner
They work at a ....

10   activities director, cook, assembler, tour guide, housekeepers, concierge, pilot
They work at a ....

Review

Directions: Read the memo and choose the one best answer (A), (B), (C) or (D) to each question.

Questions 11–14 refer to the following announcement.

> ## Memo
>
> As you know, Friday afternoon is our annual company party. We are looking forward to this event and the opportunity to take some time out of our busy schedules to enjoy each other's company. Because we will continue to need to have someone to answer the phones and receive materials, we are asking that each of our six departments identify one or more employees who would be willing to work a two-hour shift: 1:30–3:30 or 3:30–5:30.
>
> In order to compensate those people who will be working during the festivities, we have vouchers for a weekend visit to Palm Resorts. Please send me the name of the person(s) in your department who will be taking on these duties.

11 To whom is the memo directed?

(A) All employees
(B) The head of each department
(C) People at the resort
(D) The catering company

12 What is the main idea of the memo?

(A) Some lucky employees will win a trip to Palm Resorts.
(B) The party will be for all employees.
(C) Some employees will not be able to attend the party on Friday.
(D) The party will finish between 5:30 and 6:00.

13 How many people will work during the party?

(A) Fewer than five
(B) At least twelve
(C) Six or more
(D) All employees

14 What is the purpose of the event on Friday?

(A) To take as many calls as possible
(B) To motivate employees for a difficult year
(C) To get a trip to Palm Resorts
(D) To spend time with each other

Reading			
Part VII			
11	Ⓐ Ⓑ Ⓒ Ⓓ		
12	Ⓐ Ⓑ Ⓒ Ⓓ		
13	Ⓐ Ⓑ Ⓒ Ⓓ		
14	Ⓐ Ⓑ Ⓒ Ⓓ		

Chapter Three General Business & Finance

Listening comprehension PART I

Strategy A

Use the pictures to guess vocabulary. Look at the pictures and list the things you see in your head. Some things you may recognize, but some things you may not be able to name specifically. For example, in the first picture, two of the people have books. You can recognize a book from its shape, but what kind of books are they? They could be appointment books, diaries, address books, instruction manuals, etc.

What?	telephone, laptop, Post-it® Notes, sellotape, a stapler, a stamp, a computer, a chair, office workers	What?	computer screen, keyboard, mouse, mouse mat, files
Possible items	diaries, a folder	Possible items	floppy disks, client records

Task A

Identify objects

Cross out the word(s) that do NOT belong in the group.

1   check book, deposit slip, library, checks, savings account, help sign

2   weights, balance sheet, debits, linens, assets, overhead costs

3   division, stock, shares, dividends, traders, common room

4   broker, dog market, bands, bonds, bear market, risk

5   interest rates, rebate, loans, marketing, credit check, mortgage

Strategy B

The TOEIC® test often asks you to guess what is happening in the picture.
The guess may or may not be true, but based on the picture, it is likely to be true.

Look at the picture and ask yourself what you think is happening. Then read the
answer choices and compare the correct answer with the other options.
Ask yourself what part of the wrong answers could be true.

(A)	They're waiting for the television technician.	(A)	The shoppers are in the produce market.
(B)	They're relaxing in front of the TV.	(B)	The soccer fans are cheering for their team.
(C)	They're participating in a video conference.	(C)	The citizens are voting in an election.
(D)	They're watching a sports event.	(D)	Two brokers are making a trade.

The correct answer is (C). The correct answer is (D).

Task B

Identify an event

**The sentences in the left column (6–10) describe an action. The sentences in the right column (A–E)
guess what is happening. Match the actions with the guesses to identify an event.**

6	He is calculating numbers.	(A)	They are applying for a loan.
7	The woman is handing the teller some money.	(B)	The manager is preparing the budget.
8	He is giving the clerk a credit card.	(C)	The real estate agent is showing the house.
9	The group is looking at some property.	(D)	The tourist is buying U.S. dollars.
10	The couple is meeting with a bank officer.	(E)	He just purchased a stereo system.

Review 📼

Directions: Listen to the statements and choose the one that best describes what you see in the picture.

11

12

13

14

Listening Comprehension				
Part I				
11	Ⓐ	Ⓑ	Ⓒ	Ⓓ
12	Ⓐ	Ⓑ	Ⓒ	Ⓓ
13	Ⓐ	Ⓑ	Ⓒ	Ⓓ
14	Ⓐ	Ⓑ	Ⓒ	Ⓓ

PART II

Strategy A

Listen for questions and answer choices that include suggestions. The word *should* usually indicates a suggestion.

> Who *should* she contact when she gets to Paris?
> The branch manager will be able to help her.
> She could call the branch manager.
> I would contact the branch manager.

All three of the responses give suggestions. *Should* in the question indicates that a suggestion is probably necessary. Be careful, however, not all questions that include *should* are asking for suggestions, and not all questions that ask for suggestions begin with *should*.

> **Grammar Glossary** **Conditional: *should/would*** (p215)

Task A

Identify a suggestion

Read the conversations. Cross out the question if it does NOT ask for a suggestion. Underline the suggestion given in the response.

1   **A:** Who should review the preliminary budget numbers?
    B: Peju Tyler has done a great job of analyzing the budget in the past.

2   **A:** What bank should we use to finance the expansion?
    B: Let's discuss that with our accountant.

3   **A:** Should the company be opening so many new stores at the same time?
    B The President feels that they must be aggressive now.

4   **A:** How would you use the money to improve efficiency?
    B: I would spend it on additional training for the employees.

5   **A:** With lower interest rates, should we refinance our mortgage?
    B: You won't find better rates!

6   **A:** We should finish the projections by tonight, shouldn't we?
    B: Yes, unless we run into some problems.

7   **A:** How can I lower my interest rate payments?
    B: You could pay the entire balance every month.

8   **A:** How can they increase their revenue?
    B: Have they considered spending more on advertising?

9   **A:** When should we submit our requests for next year?
    B: The deadline is November 30.

10 **A:** What should I do with the budgets from 1997 and 1998?
    B: I would keep them in the locked filing cabinets in the large conference room.

Real spoken English
Words with positive meanings like *better* may not always be positive.
It is important to read the whole sentence.

Fabio could be better with details.	*means*	Fabio is not very good with details.
Hellena Products has seen better years.	*means*	This is a very bad period for Hellena Products.

Strategy B

Listen for questions that begin with *how* to identify a method of doing something.

> *How* did he finish the research?
> *How* are the workers organized?
> *How* will the managers be advised of their budgets?

Task B

Identify a method

First, underline the object in each question (11–15). Then, match the most likely method (A–E) with the question.

11	How did he do such an excellent job on that <u>report</u>?	.....*B*.....
12	How is the company able to issue more stock?	....
13	How did they improve their credit rating?	....
14	How will they attract more investors?	....
15	How was she able to make so much money in the stock market?	....

(A)   They are counting on word of mouth.
(B)   He compiled input from all of his colleagues.
(C)   Her friends think that it was all a matter of luck.
(D)   The company collected on its outstanding accounts.
(E)   There are still available shares from the initial offering.

Review 📼

Directions: Listen and choose the best response to each question.

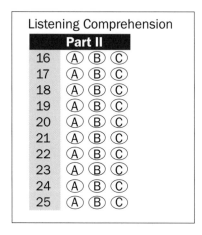

Listening Comprehension
Part II
16 Ⓐ Ⓑ Ⓒ
17 Ⓐ Ⓑ Ⓒ
18 Ⓐ Ⓑ Ⓒ
19 Ⓐ Ⓑ Ⓒ
20 Ⓐ Ⓑ Ⓒ
21 Ⓐ Ⓑ Ⓒ
22 Ⓐ Ⓑ Ⓒ
23 Ⓐ Ⓑ Ⓒ
24 Ⓐ Ⓑ Ⓒ
25 Ⓐ Ⓑ Ⓒ

PART III

Task A

Identify the performance level

**Read the sentences. Underline the part of the sentence that describes the performance level.
Then put the sentences in order from best to worst (1=best and 3=worst).**

1 (A) Luca is doing well for a beginner. ....2.....
   (B) Enzo is amazing at the job. ....
   (C) Fabio could be better with details and customer relations. ....

2 (A) Athens Food has improved considerably. ....
   (B) Hellena Products has seen better years. ....
   (C) Mykonos Desserts is having a record year. ....

3 (A) Our current economic situation can't get any worse. ....
   (B) Our revenues for fiscal year 2003 should exceed expectations. ....
   (C) The situation is beginning to look up in our Eastern markets. ....

4 (A) His investment portfolio has taken a downward turn. ....
   (B) Stock prices have been steadily climbing. ....
   (C) Her investment has tripled in value. ....

5 (A) Due to his exceptional performance he will receive a raise. ....
   (B) The marketing department is scaling back its projects. ....
   (C) As of next month, the service department will be permanently closed. ....

Strategy B

Look for questions that ask you for characteristics about a specific thing or person.

>*What* are the requirements for the job?
>*How* does their benefits package compare to others?
>*What* does the speaker say about the software program?

Task B

Identify characteristics

Cross out the answer choices that do NOT identify specific characteristics.
Then underline the words or phrases in the sentences that do identify characteristics.

6   What does the speaker say the budget process is like?
    (A) It's long and time consuming.
    (B) It's stressful.
    (C) It takes place at the same time each year.
    (D) It's headed by the senior financial analyst.

7   How do stock dividends work?
    (A) They are distributed quarterly.
    (B) They are based on company earnings.
    (C) They were sent by mistake.
    (D) They will be canceled this year.

8   What is a down payment?
    (A) It's necessary to purchase a home.
    (B) It's traditionally 20% of the total price.
    (C) It was rejected by the bank.
    (D) It shows intention to pay.

9   What does the speaker say about the loan the partners applied for?
    (A) It will be paid over a 10-year period.
    (B) It can be paid in full before its maturity date.
    (C) It was needed to build the new office.
    (D) It requires a lot of paperwork.

Review 📼

Directions: Listen and choose the best answer to each question.

10 How do the speakers rate the performance of the accounting firm?

    (A) Highly.
    (B) Not good.
    (C) Average.
    (D) Inferior.

11 What kind of hotels do they use?

    (A) Luxury.
    (B) 4-star.
    (C) Resorts.
    (D) Inexpensive.

12 Which stocks have not fallen?

    (A) Entertainment.
    (B) Medical.
    (C) Transportation.
    (D) Utility.

13 How does the woman rate the information?

    (A) She wasn't impressed with it.
    (B) She had too much time.
    (C) She thought that it was very good.
    (D) She wanted more information.

Listening Comprehension			
Part III			
10	Ⓐ Ⓑ Ⓒ Ⓓ		
11	Ⓐ Ⓑ Ⓒ Ⓓ		
12	Ⓐ Ⓑ Ⓒ Ⓓ		
13	Ⓐ Ⓑ Ⓒ Ⓓ		

PART IV

Task A

Identify a point of view

Mark an *F* next to those sentences that give factual information and an *O* next to the sentences that give an opinion.

1. (A) The lowest rate that they offer is 9%. ....*F*....
   (B) The rate is too high. ....*O*....
   (C) You should be able to get a better rate. ....*O*....

2. (A) Any complaints should be directed to Mr. Halm. ....
   (B) Not everyone will be satisfied. ....
   (C) All requests for changes need to be submitted in writing. ....

3. (A) Before being promoted, employees must have a review with a manager. ....
   (B) No one should be promoted before they have completed two years of service with the company. ....
   (C) It seems as though the promotion policy is out of date. ....

4. (A) The college sent out its catalogue to more than 20,000 interested applicants. ....
   (B) Detailed information about different fields of study is presented in the pamphlet. ....
   (C) The catalogue would be more effective in color. ....

5. (A) The list of assets should include the property acquired in the takeover. ....
   (B) The value of the assets comes to just under $20 million. ....
   (C) Although currently strong, the company should increase its amount of liquid assets. ....

6. (A) The federal government needn't be involved in the setting of rates for personal loans. ....
   (B) His chances of being approved for a loan are low. ....
   (C) He submitted his application over a month ago. ....

Strategy B

Use the questions and answers to identify a situation. Listen for questions that begin with *what*.

What is happening?
What will they do next?
What just happened?

Task B 📼

Identify the situation

Read the information below. Listen to a line from a conversation. Identify where the conversation is taking place (A–D) and what the situation is (E–H).

7	....*B*...... , ...*H*....
8	.... , ...
9	.... , ...
10	.... , ...

Location
(A) at a business meeting
(B) at a bank
(C) on the telephone
(D) at an office

Situation
(E) interviewing for a job
(F) disputing a credit card charge
(G) reviewing an annual budget
(H) applying for a loan

Review 📼

Directions: Listen and choose the best answer to each question.

11 What does the speaker want the audience to do?

(A) Invest in his factory
(B) Borrow more money
(C) Start new companies
(D) Rethink their lending policies

12 What do the analysts think about the trend?

(A) It's dangerous.
(B) It's expensive.
(C) It's normal.
(D) It's productive.

13 What is the meeting about?

(A) Workers are not taking enough vacation.
(B) Everyone is going to Thailand.
(C) People are too relaxed.
(D) Break periods are too long.

14 What does the CEO think about vacations?

(A) They're too trendy.
(B) They're necessary.
(C) They're expensive.
(D) They're inefficient.

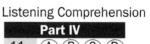

Listening Comprehension
Part IV
11 Ⓐ Ⓑ Ⓒ Ⓓ
12 Ⓐ Ⓑ Ⓒ Ⓓ
13 Ⓐ Ⓑ Ⓒ Ⓓ
14 Ⓐ Ⓑ Ⓒ Ⓓ

Reading PART V

Grammar Glossary **Parts of Speech (p217) Word Families (p221)**

Task A

Identify the correct word among the same word family

Write in the correct form of the word given in bold. Then use the list of endings to complete the other forms the base word could make.

-ion -er -or -ing -ive -ed -ity -ial -ment -ance -t -d -ier -ist

1   The company's *production* rate is expected to improve. (**produce**)
     Other forms of the word: ...*product*... (n) ...*produced*... (pp) ...*producing*.. (g) ...*producer*... (n) ...*productive*... (adj) *productivity* (n)

2   Mr. Marokovich doesn't want to .... the estimates, but he will probably have to. (**revise**)
     Other forms of the word: .... (n) .... (n) .... (g) .... (pp)

3   Her start-up company is being .... by a development agency that assists women entrepreneurs. (**finance**)
     Other forms of the word: .... (n) .... (g) .... (pp) .... (adj)

4   As a young man, he made a wise .... which made him very wealthy. (**invest**)
     Other forms of the word: .... (n) .... (g) .... (pp)

5   The city has a database of .... agencies for high-tech companies. (**lend**)
     Other forms of the word: .... (n) .... (g) .... (pp)

6   Even though their .... was not up to expectations, investors still have confidence in the company. (**perform**)
     Other forms of the word: .... (n) .... (g) .... (pp)

Strategy B

Read the sentences quickly to look for verbs. Identify the tense of the verbs. When there are multiple verbs within the same sentence, confirm that the verb tenses are logical.

> *Before he orders the materials, he reviews his inventory.*
> *Before he ordered the materials, he reviewed his inventory.*

Both of the sentences above are correct. Reading them quickly, you see two verbs: *order* and *review*. In the first sentence, both verbs are in the simple present. In the second sentence, both verbs are in the past tense.

Task B

Identify the correct sequence of tenses

Write the verb tenses in the correct phrase.
Then, put the phrases in the correct order to make a logical sentence.

7   (A) bought   (B) would have

so that he ....*B*.... a large enough supply
he ....*A*..... the extra machines

He bought the extra machines, so that he would have a large enough supply.

8   (A) suggested   (B) believes   (C) will listen

but no one .... that
the accountant .... cutting back travel expenses
management .... to the advice

....

9   (A) doesn't want to   (B) forgot

and now accounting .... reimburse her for the expenses
she .... to keep her receipts

....

10   (A) were   (B) are shocked   (C) failed

and now .... at the interest rate they have to pay
the partners .... in such a hurry to secure the loan
that they .... to read the fine print

....

11   (A) had been done   (B) finished

they .... the year so strongly
that the budget, which .... in the fall, was unrealistic

....

Review

Directions: Choose the one word or phrase that best completes the sentence.

12 The Stock Market falls when the unemployment rate ....

    (A) will rise
    (B) rises
    (C) risen
    (D) have risen

13 The company plans to issue .... for the first time next quarter.

    (A) divide
    (B) dividends
    (C) divisive
    (D) divider

14 Hix & Co. will announce sales figures from the last quarter which .... expected to be low.

    (A) will
    (B) is
    (C) are
    (D) were

15 It is up to the head of the division to use the .... funds.

    (A) discretionary
    (B) discreet
    (C) discretion
    (D) discreetly

16 His budget always tends to be .... , which protects his department from unexpected costs.

    (A) inflation
    (B) inflationary
    (C) inflate
    (D) inflated

Reading				
Part V				
12	Ⓐ	Ⓑ	Ⓒ	Ⓓ
13	Ⓐ	Ⓑ	Ⓒ	Ⓓ
14	Ⓐ	Ⓑ	Ⓒ	Ⓓ
15	Ⓐ	Ⓑ	Ⓒ	Ⓓ
16	Ⓐ	Ⓑ	Ⓒ	Ⓓ

PART VI

Strategy A

When you see a pronoun underlined in this section of the TOEIC test, check that it is the correct pronoun for the noun that it is referring to. Then make sure that the correct form of that pronoun is used.

> When the company went public, all of *its* records were made available to the public.

The pronoun *its* refers to the noun *company*. The possessive form of the pronoun is correct for this sentence.

> After the financial records were publicized, *it* was criticized for being vague and incomplete.

In this case, the wrong pronoun is used. This is a common error on the TOEIC test. *Financial records* is a plural noun, therefore the pronoun used should be *they*. The sentence should read:

> After the financial records were publicized, *they* were criticized for being vague and incomplete.

Grammar Glossary **Pronouns (p218)**

Task A

Identify the correct pronouns

Underline the correct form of the pronoun.

1   Mary met *she / her* new supervisor and the rest of *she / her* staff at the retreat.

2   The government announced the plan to open *it / its* archives to the public.

3   The employees worked all night to finish *they / their* presentation.

4   Michael is good at math so *he / him* can easily read a financial statement.

5   The prize will go to the division that has earned *it / its*.

Strategy B

Look out for incorrect determiners, which always precede nouns in a sentence. First, check if the noun is singular or plural, and a count or non-count noun. Then, check if the correct determiner is used.

Determiner	Example
Indefinite article	*a, an*
Definite article	*the*
Demonstratives	*this, that, these, those*
Possessives	*my, his, Sharon's, the schools'*
Quantity words	*many, some, each*
Numerals	*one, second*

> Grammar glossary **Adjectives: Determiners (p212)**

Task B

Identify determiners

Underline the correct form of the determiner.

6   *My / The* Mexican stock exchange has had a number of dramatic swings *this / the* year.

7   *A / Some* government laid off 20,000 state telecommunications workers when *those / the* system was privatized.

8   Mary set up a meeting with the budget director to try to increase *her / Mary's* departments' allocation.

9   The financial services company announced that it would open *that / three* new offices this year.

10 *Some / An* Internet company sold *this / its* shares for 150 yen.

Review

Directions: Identify the one underlined word or phrase that should be corrected or rewritten.

11 <u>Finishing the year</u> at 20% under budget, <u>many work team</u> won an
        A   B

    <u>all-expenses-paid</u> trip to <u>an ocean resort</u>.
        C   D

12 Their <u>recommending</u> was <u>to cut</u> the staff if <u>its performance</u> did not improve <u>soon</u>.
           A   B   C   D

13 <u>The number of people</u> using credit cards <u>has increased</u> <u>dramatically</u> in <u>last third months</u>.
          A   B   C   D

14 Silvio and Anh <u>should be able</u> to finish all the work <u>by tomorrow</u> if <u>their</u> not <u>interrupted</u>.
                  A   B   C   D

15 Because of <u>these</u> year's abundant crop, High Time Coffee <u>has announced</u> that <u>it</u> will cut <u>its prices</u>.
             A   B   C   D

16 The president announced <u>at the meeting</u> that <u>him</u> attempts to raise
                                  A   B

    <u>additional funds</u> for the expansion <u>had failed</u>.
        C   D

17 <u>The recent acquisition</u> has made <u>it</u> necessary <u>to change</u> <u>a companies'</u> accounting systems.
          A   B   C   D

18 Rident Automotive now <u>offers</u> a <u>number of payment plans</u> for <u>their</u> <u>preferred customers</u>.
                        A   B   C   D

19 When <u>a</u> chief executive officer <u>announced</u> that she <u>would be resigning</u>
          A   B   C

    immediately, the stock price <u>fell sharply</u>.
                              D

20 <u>To increase</u> our company's <u>security</u>, all of <u>a</u> financial records
        A   B   C

    are kept in <u>an</u> undisclosed secure place.
              D

Reading

Part VI				
11	Ⓐ	Ⓑ	Ⓒ	Ⓓ
12	Ⓐ	Ⓑ	Ⓒ	Ⓓ
13	Ⓐ	Ⓑ	Ⓒ	Ⓓ
14	Ⓐ	Ⓑ	Ⓒ	Ⓓ
15	Ⓐ	Ⓑ	Ⓒ	Ⓓ
16	Ⓐ	Ⓑ	Ⓒ	Ⓓ
17	Ⓐ	Ⓑ	Ⓒ	Ⓓ
18	Ⓐ	Ⓑ	Ⓒ	Ⓓ
19	Ⓐ	Ⓑ	Ⓒ	Ⓓ
20	Ⓐ	Ⓑ	Ⓒ	Ⓓ

PART VII

> We regret to inform you that we will be forced to cancel your credit card if we do not receive payment within the next 15 days. The balance on your account has been outstanding for over 90 days. While we value you as an important customer, we cannot overlook this. Until we receive payment, you will be unable to use your card. Upon payment, you will once again be able to enjoy all the benefits of being a cardholder.

(D) is the correct answer. The word *first* in the question indicates that you need to identify a sequence of events. (A) This is something that the *sender* will do, not the *recipient*. (B) This refers to a past event – the 90-day lateness of payment. It is not something that anyone *should do*. (C) Contacting the company sounds logical, but it is not mentioned in the notice. (D) The recipient should make payment within the next 15 days. Therefore (D) is the correct answer.

Task A

Identify the sequence of events

Read a sentence from a passage and choose the best answer.

1   Following the intense and prolonged negotiations, she took a three-week vacation.
What happened first?

(A) She went on vacation.
(B) She finished the negotiations.
(C) She prolonged the negotiations.

2   In order to make accurate predictions, they must first have the historical data and the competitor's information.
When is it possible to make good predictions?

(A) When they have both types of data
(B) After they get the historical data
(C) Before they have the competitor's information

3   If the company doesn't invest in a new computer system soon, it won't be able to produce accurate reports with the tremendous amount of information it is receiving.
What should the company do immediately?

(A) Purchase a new system
(B) Get more information
(C) Publish the reports

4   Before we begin making any final changes, everyone should go back and check the figures that have been submitted.
What should be done now?

(A) Everyone should change their numbers.
(B) They should verify the numbers.
(C) The final product should be determined.

Strategy B

Look for questions that include words such as *must*, *need to*, and *necessary* to identify questions that ask for requirements. Often requirements are listed together. Questions about requirements are very specific, so you can read the passage quickly to locate exactly the information that is asked for.

What *must* employees do before the training session?
What does the group *need to* submit to the bank official?
What items are *necessary* for a successful opening?

What must the reader do if she is interested?
(A)   Have access to a computer
(B)   Wait a short period of time
(C)   Establish good credit
(D)   Give the names of some people she knows

Technological changes have made it easier for individuals to take charge of their personal finances. Now you can access all of the information you need, in just minutes!
Join **FinaForm Infoquest** and secure your future now.

At **FinaForm Infoquest** you can access the lowest finance rates for houses, automobiles, even college education! You can enter the stock market, assisted by our expert traders. You can invest in bonds and mutual funds. All of this access is available to you at a very low cost, and it is easier than you think. All you need to do is to provide us with a statement of annual income, two credit references, and a list of four friends or acquaintances who might be interested in our services. Don't delay, call today!

(D) is the correct answer. The question asks for requirements. You should read the passage quickly and look for the section where the requirements are listed. You see the word *need* and a list at the end of the passage, so you will likely find requirements listed here. (A) This is never mentioned in the passage, although you might connect technological changes with computers. (B) *Time* is referred to at the beginning of the passage, but *waiting* is not one of the requirements. (C) *Credit* is mentioned at the end of the passage, where the requirements are listed. However, the passage doesn't say what kind of credit history is needed. (D) The *names of people* refers to *friends and acquaintances*, so this option is the correct answer.

Task B

Identify requirements

Cross out the words that are NOT a requirement for the item underlined.

5   loan application
     bank statement, curriculum vitae, identification, education, annual income, credit references

6   credit card
     phone number, height, tax bracket, billing address, credit history, debt

7   annual report
     overall performance, projections, Board of Directors, gross sales, paychecks, invoice

8   weekly meeting
     agenda, attendance, minutes, hiring manual, leader, waiting period

9   budgets
     low prices, allocation of funds, employee salaries, interest rates, housing loan, estimates

10   balance sheet
     assets, letter of recommendation, company background, debits, liabilities, legal assistance

Review

Directions: Read the memo and choose the one best answer (A), (B), (C) or (D) to each question.

Questions 11–14 refer to the following memo.

> *To*:   Department Heads
> *From*: Charlene Boyer, CEO
> *Date*: August 1
>
> It's that time of year again! Many of you have already begun work on your department's budget for next year. In an attempt to make the process smoother and more satisfactory for everyone involved, we are making some changes to the process.
>
> As usual, department heads are asked to submit preliminary budgets to the Executive Committee by August 15. This year, we want to involve more employees in the process. A special committee will review the budgets. This committee will consist of four members of the Executive Committee and two representatives from each department.
>
> As department heads, you will choose your own representatives to the committee. They must be able to contribute 10 hours a week for a month. Please submit their names by August 7.

11   What is required of the representatives?

(A) They must be a member of the Executive Committee.
(B) They must submit a budget by August 15.
(C) They must be the department head.
(D) They must be willing to spend 40 hours on this project in one month.

12   How does Ms. Boyer feel about the budget process?

(A) Only the top management should be involved.
(B) It can't be improved.
(C) It should be a more open process.
(D) It's time to finalize the budget.

13   Who decided on the budgets last year?

(A) Departments, through democratic vote
(B) Representatives from each department
(C) The Executive Committee
(D) The department heads

14   What will happen next?

(A) A list of names will be given to Ms. Boyer.
(B) The initial budgets will be turned in.
(C) The Executive Committee will meet.
(D) The process will be smoother.

Reading

	Part VII			
11	Ⓐ	Ⓑ	Ⓒ	Ⓓ
12	Ⓐ	Ⓑ	Ⓒ	Ⓓ
13	Ⓐ	Ⓑ	Ⓒ	Ⓓ
14	Ⓐ	Ⓑ	Ⓒ	Ⓓ

Chapter Four Housing & Property

Listening comprehension PART I

Strategy A

Use the pictures to identify physical relationships. Look at the pictures carefully and ask yourself *where* an object is in relation to another object or person.

Where?
The contractor is holding a pipe in his right hand.
The contractor is holding the plans in his left hand.

Where?
The sign is next to the sidewalk.
The sign is at the edge of the lawn.

Grammar Glossary Prepositions of Location (p218)

Task A

Identify the physical relationship between objects

Underline the correct preposition to describe the most probable relationship between the objects.

1   The doorknob is *on / in* the right side of the glass door.

2   The housekeeper pointed to the broken window *above / on top of* the sofa.

3   The apartment was located *near / within* a bus stop.

4   The building manager took out the keys which were hidden *under / in front of* the desk in a small drawer.

5   The crane is sitting directly *in front of / around* our offices.

Strategy B

Be aware of answer choices that are irrelevant. The TOEIC® test often uses answer choices that are not relevant to the photo. Make a quick mental list of what you see in the pictures. In the first picture below this might include: *blueprints, papers, drawings, people, architects, engineers*. Look for related vocabulary in the answer choices. Ask yourself what parts of the wrong answers are relevant and what parts are irrelevant.

(A)   She's cutting lumber for a house.
(B)   The building is underground.
(C)   She's discussing the plans.
(D)   They're buying new hard hats.

The correct answer is (C).

(A)   The painter is sanding the walls.
(B)   The plumber is fixing the leak.
(C)   The electrician is wiring the ceiling.
(D)   The carpenter is on the roof.

The correct answer is (D).

Task B

Identify irrelevancies

Cross out the word that is NOT related to all of the other words. Tell why.

6   screw, hammer, screwdriver, hardware store, nail
....

7   wall, ceiling, carpet, door, window
....

8   ladder, wheelbarrow, scaffold, crane, stairs
....

9   constructing, building, erecting, demolishing, putting up
....

10   owning, renting, leasing, hiring, letting
....

Review

Directions: Listen to the statements and choose the one that best describes what you see in the picture.

11

12

13

管 理 地

お問い合せ先

神田土地建物株式会社

千代田区西神田1丁目3番地6号

TEL 3291-5011(代表)

14

Listening Comprehension

Part I				
11	Ⓐ	Ⓑ	Ⓒ	Ⓓ
12	Ⓐ	Ⓑ	Ⓒ	Ⓓ
13	Ⓐ	Ⓑ	Ⓒ	Ⓓ
14	Ⓐ	Ⓑ	Ⓒ	Ⓓ

PART II

Listen for questions that ask *what* to identify things.

What is the man looking at?
What is the problem with the building?
What does the woman have in her hands?
What delayed the construction?

Task A

Identify things

Cross out the answer choices that are NOT possible.

1   What is the man carrying?

    (A) I believe it is the ladder.
    (B) It is a tape measure.
    (C) He has a hard-hat on his head.

2   What is behind the office?

    (A) An adjoining office.
    (B) There is nothing there yet.
    (C) The store is in front.

3   What is being stored next to the supplies?

    (A) They belong to the previous owner.
    (B) Just an old computer.
    (C) There is nothing there right now.

4   What is the going rate for new property in this area?

    (A) The prices vary greatly.
    (B) It's approximately $3.50 per square foot.
    (C) The vacancy level is very high.

5   What equipment does she need for her work?

    (A) She made a lot of money last year.
    (B) It varies from project to project.
    (C) A drafting table and some good pencils.

6   What is the problem with the new lights?

    (A) The switch doesn't work properly.
    (B) They were installed over a month ago.
    (C) The wires were crossed by accident.

7   What is next on her agenda?

    (A) A brief meeting and then lunch.
    (B) She is planning to visit the site.
    (C) The agents were pleased with the visits.

8   What are the superintendent's main responsibilities?

    (A) He doesn't earn enough.
    (B) Taking care of all of the units and overseeing the staff.
    (C) Maintenance, repairs and general assistance.

9   What is causing the delay?

    (A) The materials haven't arrived.
    (B) They will commence work at 1:00.
    (C) There is a bad accident on the highway.

10 What is the main problem with the old facility?

    (A) They say that it is valued at over $5 million.
    (B) The plumbing can't be used any longer.
    (C) It has extensive water damage from the flood last year.

Listen for questions that ask for the status of a situation.
The status indicates whether something is finished, being worked on, postponed, forgotten, etc.

> *Is* the project *finished*?
> *When will* they sign the lease?
> Why *is she making another* trip to the new facilities?

Task B

Identify the status of the situation

Mark the sentences that indicate a situation that is finished with a *F*, a situation that is being worked on with a *WO* and others with an *O*.

11   (A)   The president stopped the project after he saw the initial plans. ....*O*....
        (B)   That was wrapped up last week. ...*F*......
        (C)   They want to finalize everything before the construction begins. ...*WO*...

12   (A)   All of the art was hung last night. ....
        (B)   There are five remaining pieces to arrange. ....
        (C)   Unfortunately, that project was pushed to the back of the line. ....

13   (A)   They've been working all day on a final decision. ....
        (B)   In a vote of five to four, the project was approved. ....
        (C)   Although the deadline is tomorrow, they only started discussions yesterday. ....

14   (A)   The bank has been analyzing the company's credit history for the building loan. ....
        (B)   The bank went out of business while they were in the process of reviewing the application. ....
        (C)   The records say that that file was closed months ago. ....

15   (A)   By granting the final seal of approval, they were finally able to put the building behind them. ....
        (B)   We've sent the plans to the contractor's office and they're dealing with them. ....
        (C)   They were unable to come to a consensus. ....

Review 🔊

Directions: Listen and choose the best response to each question.

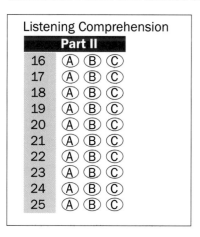

Listening Comprehension		
Part II		
16	Ⓐ Ⓑ Ⓒ	
17	Ⓐ Ⓑ Ⓒ	
18	Ⓐ Ⓑ Ⓒ	
19	Ⓐ Ⓑ Ⓒ	
20	Ⓐ Ⓑ Ⓒ	
21	Ⓐ Ⓑ Ⓒ	
22	Ⓐ Ⓑ Ⓒ	
23	Ⓐ Ⓑ Ⓒ	
24	Ⓐ Ⓑ Ⓒ	
25	Ⓐ Ⓑ Ⓒ	

PART III

Task A

Identify a recommendation or suggestion

Listen to a conversation and check the choice that best finishes the conversation with an appropriate suggestion or recommendation.

1. (A) Why don't you send a memo about it?
   (B) It shouldn't take more than four months.
   (C) I would start looking again.
   (D) He has had problems before with his vision.

2. (A) You should verify the type of payment.
   (B) We bought fifteen just last week.
   (C) You might think about renting.
   (D) Why don't you find a music group?

3. (A) Area commercial property should increase in price.
   (B) The downtown area is undergoing a renovation.
   (C) Let's redecorate.
   (D) It's time to start looking for new space.

4. (A) I have to leave in a couple of minutes.
   (B) Rob is the new owner.
   (C) You should try to attend. It's important.
   (D) You can tell me about it tomorrow.

5. (A) The last group bought a lot of merchandise.
   (B) I would invite them back next week.
   (C) We should increase the asking price.
   (D) It would be better to show them one at a time.

Strategy B

Look for questions that ask to identify a request.
Look for questions that begin with *what*. Make sure you choose the request for the correct speaker.

> *What* does the woman want the man to do?
> *What* will the speaker request?
> *What* did the customer ask for?

Task B

Identify requests

Listen to a line from a conversation. Then underline the answer choice that correctly identifies the request.

6   What is the labor union asking for?

   (A) It is always changing.
   (B) They want better medical benefits and higher salaries.
   (C) The man doesn't know.
   (D) It is asking for more help.

7   What is the speaker requesting?

   (A) Material to mail to clients.
   (B) The right to hang up notices.
   (C) Larger offices.
   (D) Lower mail rates.

8   What is being requested?

   (A) A lowering of the rent.
   (B) An extension of the lease.
   (C) A deduction in the yearly payments.
   (D) More space.

9   What is the city requesting?

   (A) A measurement of the site.
   (B) Early completion of the project.
   (C) Removal of all the debris.
   (D) A listing of all materials.

Review

Directions: Listen and choose the best answer to each question.

10   What have the developers requested?

   (A) A revised budget.
   (B) A meeting with the speaker.
   (C) Another month to work.
   (D) More time to finish.

11   What does the woman recommend doing?

   (A) Resubmitting the building permit.
   (B) Pushing the builder a bit.
   (C) Asking the mayor to help.
   (D) Taking longer to build.

12   What is the man's recommendation?

   (A) To work less hours.
   (B) To change her appearance.
   (C) To walk from home.
   (D) To resubmit her request.

13   What does the woman ask Nicole to do?

   (A) Pay the bill.
   (B) Call the electricity company.
   (C) Find the bill.
   (D) Buy a calculator.

Listening Comprehension			
Part III			
10	Ⓐ	Ⓑ Ⓒ Ⓓ
11	Ⓐ	Ⓑ Ⓒ Ⓓ
12	Ⓐ	Ⓑ Ⓒ Ⓓ
13	Ⓐ	Ⓑ Ⓒ Ⓓ

PART IV

Task A

Identify the problem

Listen to three talks. Before each talk begins, read the answer choices quickly.
Then cross out the answer choices that are NOT possible.

1 Why are they meeting?

   (A) To solve a problem.
   (B) To create a plan of action.
   (C) To complain to the city council.
   (D) To reduce the number of criminals.

2 What is the problem?

   (A) There are fewer cinemas.
   (B) Robberies and homicides have increased.
   (C) There are too many buyers.
   (D) Frightened people don't buy property.

3 What is the purpose of the advertisement?

   (A) To raise interest in commercial space.
   (B) To announce full-occupancy.
   (C) To entice buyers.
   (D) To promote an office complex.

4 What is the problem?

   (A) Space is limited.
   (B) No more appointments are available.
   (C) Offices are only for rent.
   (D) Time is short.

5 Why have the people gathered?

   (A) They want to go swimming.
   (B) They rented an apartment on the third floor.
   (C) They want to tour an apartment complex.
   (D) They are interested in a place to live.

6 What is a drawback to the complex?

   (A) There are only three floors.
   (B) It is under construction.
   (C) There are no recreational facilities.
   (D) The swimming pool isn't ready yet.

Strategy B

Use the questions and answers to identify solutions to problems. Remember that solutions generally come after the problem has been identified.

Due to low attendance, we will reschedule the meeting for next month. Details will be sent to you in the mail. We apologize for any inconveniences.

The problem isn't stated directly in the sentences above, but you can guess that the problem is that they had to cancel a meeting. The problem is referred to *due to low attendance* and is followed by a solution *we will reschedule*.

Task B 📼

Identify possible solutions

Listen to four talks and identify possible solutions. Cross out the answer choices that do NOT present possible solutions.

7
(A) The police department will not listen to a group of realtors.
(B) The realtors can submit individual plans.
(C) The realtors invite criminals to help them.
(D) The plan demands more police on the street.

8
(A) There'll always be another chance.
(B) More than one hundred offices can still be built.
(C) 30% of the space is still available.
(D) Appointments can still be made.

9
(A) People can go to a nearby gym to use a pool.
(B) They can park at a local facility.
(C) Tenants may rent a three-bedroom apartment.
(D) Most tenants don't want to swim now anyway.

10
(A) Roads will not be repaired.
(B) Property tax will be increased.
(C) A committee will study the problem.
(D) The Council will close the schools.

Test Note
Once you identify a problem, you should anticipate possible solutions. Don't, however, choose an answer that is not mentioned in the talk. In order for the answer to be correct, it must be stated or inferred in the listening.

Review 📼

Directions: Listen and choose the best answer to each question.

11 What problem do the managers have?
(A) They don't know how to manage.
(B) They don't have enough time.
(C) They aren't making any money.
(D) They can't keep employees busy.

12 How can the speaker help?
(A) By giving low-cost loans.
(B) By finding good properties.
(C) By providing office managers.
(D) By referring other business.

13 Why is the speaker making the announcement?
(A) To present a plan of action.
(B) To announce a retirement package.
(C) To congratulate a good painter.
(D) To improve morale.

14 What does the speaker suggest everyone do?
(A) Work independently.
(B) Go to the marina.
(C) Take no vacation for the next 14 days.
(D) Take some time off.

Listening Comprehension			
Part IV			
11	Ⓐ Ⓑ Ⓒ Ⓓ		
12	Ⓐ Ⓑ Ⓒ Ⓓ		
13	Ⓐ Ⓑ Ⓒ Ⓓ		
14	Ⓐ Ⓑ Ⓒ Ⓓ		

Strategy A

Look at the sentence to identify the cause of a problem and its effect.

> *Cause*   *Effect*
> Due to severe economic conditions, twice the number of properties over last year are for sale.

Grammar Glossary Cause and Effect (p213)

Task A

Identify cause and effect

Mark *C* over the phrase or clause that is the cause, and *E* over the phrase or clause that is the effect.

1   The group of realtors wasn't able to sell the buildings, because of the structural faults that were discovered.

2   During the emergency training, the building complex is evacuated after the water main breaks and the bundle of loose wires catches on fire.

3   The quality of our properties improves constantly because of the intense level of competition in the surrounding areas.

4   Because of a shortage of office space, rents were very high.

5   Snow was not cleared from the parking lot, because the snow plough was being repaired.

6   Due to the unusually cold weather, the management turned on the heat.

Strategy B

Identify the verbs in the sentence and mark *S* if they are stative or *NS* if they are non-stative. Stative verbs usually do not take the progressive (-*ing*) form.

> It .... from their discussions as though the earliest date for the contract to be signed is November 25.
> (A)   is sounding
> (B)   sounding
> (C)   sound
> (D)   sounds

The correct answer is (D). You can quickly see from the answer choices that the verb to be used is *sound*. *Sound* is a stative verb and therefore does not take the progressive form. Therefore you can quickly eliminate answer choices (A) and (B). You see that with *it*, you need the third person singular -*s*, so that answer choice (C) can also be eliminated.

Grammar Glossary   Verbs: Stative   (p219)

Task B

Identify stative verbs

Check the grammatically correct sentence. Mark *S* by the stative verbs or *NS* by the non-stative verbs.

S

7   (A)   It *seems* that the executive committee liked the plans for the expansion. ✓

(B)   It *is seeming* that the executive committee likes the plans for the expansion.

8   (A)   Developers *are appearing* more and more frequently at the city council meetings.

(B)   Developers *appear* more and more frequently at the city council meetings.

9   (A)   Even though he is exhausted, he *is working* all night to finish the project.

(B)   Even though he is exhausted, he *works* all night to finish the project.

10   (A)   Even though the deal fell through, the project manager *was sensing* that another deal was possible.

(B)   Even though the deal fell through, the project manager *sensed* that another deal was possible.

11   (A)   We *are wanting* to give you a tour of the property if you are interested.

(B)   We *want* to give you a tour of the property if you are interested.

Review

Directions: Choose the one word or phrase that best completes the sentence.

12 Her finishing our design plans .... on her other projects.
   (A) is depending
   (B) depend
   (C) depends
   (D) is depended

13 The owners, by signing the agreement, ... to the neighborhood renovation project.
   (A) is committing
   (B) commits
   (C) commit
   (D) are committing

14 The new manager .... to the east coast.
   (A) are transfer
   (B) is transferring
   (C) transfers
   (D) are transferring

15 Fifteen hundred pounds of cement .... to arrive tomorrow for the housing project.
   (A) are
   (B) am
   (C) being
   (D) is

16 The lawyer, but not the client, ... that the lease is fair.
   (A) is feeling
   (B) feels
   (C) feel
   (D) are feeling

Reading				
Part V				
12	Ⓐ	Ⓑ	Ⓒ	Ⓓ
13	Ⓐ	Ⓑ	Ⓒ	Ⓓ
14	Ⓐ	Ⓑ	Ⓒ	Ⓓ
15	Ⓐ	Ⓑ	Ⓒ	Ⓓ
16	Ⓐ	Ⓑ	Ⓒ	Ⓓ

PART VI

Strategy A

When you see a gerund or an infinitive in a sentence, ask yourself which is required. Some verbs are followed by a gerund, while others are followed by an infinitive. Yet others may be followed by either.

>   She couldn't *imagine living* in the house by herself when her husband passed away. (Correct)
>   She couldn't *imagine to live* in the house by herself after her husband passed away. (Incorrect)

Remember: Some verbs can be followed by *either* a gerund or an infinitive.
>   He *remembered asking* the building manager about the availability.
>   He *remembered to ask* the building manager about the availability.

In the examples above, both sentences are correct. However, they do have different meanings, depending on the form.

Grammar Glossary Gerunds and Infinitives (p215)

Task A

Identify the appropriate use of the gerund or the infinitive

Underline the correct form of the verb.

1   The bank advised the property owners *giving / to give* an accurate appraisal of the property.

2   The landlord expected *to receive / receiving* the rent checks on the first of the month.

3   The rental agent hopes *to convince / convincing* the client that other renters want the property.

4   They are considering *bringing in / to bring in* additional staff to manage the property during the peak summer months.

5   The chairman wanted *stopping / to stop* cost overruns.

Strategy B

Look out for conjunctions and commas to indicate phrases. If you identify a series of phrases, make sure that a parallel structure (all nouns, all prepositional phrases, etc.) is used.

The firm was unable to *design the plans* and *construct the building* in the given time-frame.

The conjunction *and* connects two verb phrases, *design the plans* and *construct the building*. These phrases use a parallel structure. Note that both verbs are in the base form.

> **Grammar Glossary Parallel Structures (p216)**

Task B

Identify the parallel structures

Mark *C* over the conjunction and write the type of phrases used (noun, adjective or prepositional phrase). Then underline the phrase that does not follow the parallel structure.

6   The zoning regulations state that restaurants, <u>office build</u>, and any other
                                                        C

   commerical properties are strictly prohibited in the area. ......*noun phrases*......

7   Some of the special features include exercise facilitation on the premises, dry-
   cleaning services, and a convenience store. ....

8   Stage three required finishing touches the walls, on the restrooms and above
   the entrances and exits. ....

9   We suggested that they place the "For Rent" signs on the windows, front lawn
   or at the coffee shop. ....

10   The combination of the new airport, increased traffic, and rising crime rated
   have resulted in lower property values. ....

11   The rates for the office space included water and gas but not electrify.
   ....

12   I hate to cancel our appointment, but I can only show the property in the
   evening or the weekend. ....

13   The realtor described the apartment as open, bright and sun. ....

14   Our corporate exercise program includes strength building, aerobic training
   and weights. ....

15   The downtown properties tend to be small, dark and depression in comparison
   to the bright and open suburban properties. ....

Review

Directions: Identify the one underlined word or phrase that should be corrected or rewritten.

16 Attempt to meet his quota for the month, he made an appointment with one last client.
     A   B   C   D

17 Their bid on the house and the office spacing fell through at the last minute
            A   B   C
when a higher offer was received.
                D

18 Either the electrician or the contracting will contact you regarding
   A   B   C
the remaining work that needs to be done.
                D

19 The conference room, the outside pool area or lobby would all be
                 A   B
large enough to fit 75 guests comfortably.
      C   D

20 We'd rather be negotiate with her for a better deal, but she has been too busy with the acquisition.
              A   B   C   D

21 Easily access and affordability were the two choices that she gave the artist while looking at studios.
    A   B   C   D

22 All of the tenants were relieved to see them move out voluntarily before to be evicted by the owners.
             A   B   C   D

23 Before the painting is begun, maintenance has to repair the sprinkling system, the wiring and the plumber.
            A   B   C   D

24 There are regulations concerning the color of the buildings or the type of plants placed on balconies.
               A   B   C   D

25 After long and difficulty discussions, we decided that selling the house was the most logical answer.
      A   B   C   D

Reading

Part VI

16	Ⓐ	Ⓑ	Ⓒ	Ⓓ
17	Ⓐ	Ⓑ	Ⓒ	Ⓓ
18	Ⓐ	Ⓑ	Ⓒ	Ⓓ
19	Ⓐ	Ⓑ	Ⓒ	Ⓓ
20	Ⓐ	Ⓑ	Ⓒ	Ⓓ
21	Ⓐ	Ⓑ	Ⓒ	Ⓓ
22	Ⓐ	Ⓑ	Ⓒ	Ⓓ
23	Ⓐ	Ⓑ	Ⓒ	Ⓓ
24	Ⓐ	Ⓑ	Ⓒ	Ⓓ
25	Ⓐ	Ⓑ	Ⓒ	Ⓓ

PART VII

Realtors Plus is a monthly publication aimed at
serving the needs of the local realtor community.
Our job requires us to work intensely with our
customers and leaves us little time to work with our
colleagues. Many of us view our colleagues not as
colleagues, but as competition. Our aim is to
change that attitude and create a true community,
whereby all of us can benefit and grow our
businesses. We accomplish this aim by focusing on
market research, inside tips, and providing a "Best
Practices" feature section.

Realtors Plus will begin publication in July. It will
also be available on line the fifth of every month.
You may subscribe at www.realtorsplus.com for a
low monthly fee of $6.50. Come join our community!

The correct answer is (C). In order to answer this question correctly, you need
to understand the overall aim of the notice. While realtors often work with first-
time homebuyers, the advertisement does not mention or address these buyers,
so (A) does not answer the question. (B) refers vaguely to *aggressive competitors*.
This notice specifically refers to the opportunity for building relationships as
colleagues, not as competitors, so (B) is incorrect. (D) repeats the word
community from the notice, but this is not the targeted reader of the
advertisement. The ad is a sales notice for a new publication serving the needs
of the *local realtor community*.

Task A

Identify the target audience

Choose the answer choice that identifies the most probable target audience.

1   You're reading a notice about an eviction. Who is the likely target audience?

  (A) The burglars
  (B) The apartment manager
  (C) The tenants
  (D) A national politician

2   You're reading a report on dropping occupancy rates in the city. Who is the likely target audience?

  (A) Prospective buyers
  (B) Farmers
  (C) Hotel owners
  (D) Busy groups

3   You're reading a letter outlining problems in the building such as garbage removal, water leaks, and excessive noise. Who is the likely target audience?

  (A) Home owners
  (B) A building superintendent
  (C) The city council
  (D) An environmental group

4   You are reading an advertisement for an apartment building security device? Who is the likely target audience?

  (A) The military
  (B) A corporate operations manager
  (C) An apartment renter
  (D) A security company

Strategy B

Read the answer choices and passage quickly to look for adjectives and details to identify an event or an activity.

> What event is being announced?
> (A)   A discussion about scheduling
> (B)   Interviews to find new managers
> (C)   An international bazaar
> (D)   A meeting of managers

> Mark your calendars now if you haven't already for the semi-annual gathering of our top managers from around the world. For those of you who have attended the meeting in the past, you know the preparation that we put into the meeting and the value and information that you take away from it. For those of you for whom this will be the first meeting, welcome and congratulations!
>
> We are very careful in our selection process. Each manager must be nominated from a group of peers and supervisors. In addition, each manager has at least a 20% growth record for the past three years. Your inclusion to this year's meeting is to be congratulated.

(D) is the correct answer. Looking at the question and the answer choices, you see that you are trying to identify an event. (A) plays on the first sentence in the notice, *Mark your calendars*. However, readers are asked to mark their calendars in order to remember the meeting, not because the meeting is for scheduling purposes. (B) mentions managers, as does the passage, but there is no mention of hiring new managers. (C) uses the word *international*, which is similar in meaning to *around the world* in the passage. However, the notice is not about a bazaar. The passage is announcing a gathering, or meeting, of managers, so (D) is the correct answer.

Task B

Identify the activity or event

Cross out the answer choices that do NOT describe what might be included in the event or activity.

5   Open House

(A)   The public is invited.
(B)   Apartments are available to view.
(C)   The families in 2D and 5C changed apartments.
(D)   The restaurant closed its doors.

6   A seminar on finding the best vendors for property managers

(A)   A list of companies in the area
(B)   Good and bad examples
(C)   Services an electrician should provide
(D)   The hours for the exercise facilities

7   Auction of public lands

(A)   Held on Saturday, April 25, at 10:00 a.m.
(B)   Free for the first ten customers
(C)   Great prices
(D)   Photos of antiques

8   New tax laws

(A)   Costly political campaign
(B)   Commercial property in residential area
(C)   Intense public debate
(D)   Increased airport taxes

9   A training session for the housekeeping staff

(A)   Owners discuss new properties.
(B)   Everyone must read the safety manual.
(C)   A new childcare center opened on Main Street.
(D)   New cleaning materials have been purchased.

10   A workshop on housing changes

(A)   Construction of single family units has been stopped.
(B)   The subway system has lessened traffic.
(C)   The city is undergoing a revitalization.
(D)   New homeowners can qualify for loans.

Review

Directions: Read the announcement and choose the one best answer (A), (B), (C) or (D) to each question.

Questions 11–14 refer to the following announcement.

There will be a town meeting at the Wetlands on Manchester Blvd. on Saturday at 9:00 a.m. We encourage all citizens to get involved in the community and to attend the meeting. Speakers from the development company and environmental groups will be discussing the pros and cons of the proposed industrial and residential areas.

The City Manager's Office will be taking up the issue of development in sessions beginning next month. Before that happens, we feel that the community needs to be well-informed so that we can, in turn, guide our leaders in the action that they take. The future of our community very much depends on the outcome of this current debate.

Breakfast will be served. We ask everyone to bring a list of questions and concerns to be presented to the speakers. We look forward to seeing you there. Remember, our community's future is in your hands!

11 Who should attend the meeting?

(A) Residents on Manchester Boulevard
(B) Out-of-state tourists
(C) A building contractor
(D) All the community members

12 What will probably happen at the meeting?

(A) One invited speaker will make a presentation.
(B) City leaders will decide how many buildings to allow.
(C) Presenters will give different points of view.
(D) All new building will be prohibited.

13 When will the city leaders consider development?

(A) They will decide at 9:00 a.m. on Saturday.
(B) They have already decided.
(C) In the next thirty days or so.
(D) Immediately after the meeting.

14 Why should the local residents go to the meeting?

(A) For breakfast and to meet their neighbors
(B) To join an environmental group
(C) To elect officials
(D) To help decide the future of their community

Reading				
Part VII				
11	Ⓐ	Ⓑ	Ⓒ	Ⓓ
12	Ⓐ	Ⓑ	Ⓒ	Ⓓ
13	Ⓐ	Ⓑ	Ⓒ	Ⓓ
14	Ⓐ	Ⓑ	Ⓒ	Ⓓ

Listening comprehension PART I

Strategy A

Use the pictures to identify a situation. Ask yourself *who* is doing *what*, *where*.

Who?	The officer is on the bridge of the ship.
What?	He's looking through binoculars.
Where?	The ship is heading out to sea.

Who?	The passenger is being served by the flight attendant.
What?	The flight attendant is offering the passenger some refreshments.
Where?	The passenger is sitting on the aisle.

Task A

Identify a situation

Match the ends of the sentences (A–E) with the beginnings (1–5) to make a situation.

1 The airline sales agent behind the counter ....

2 The pilot is checking the instruments ....

3 The purser is helping the passengers ....

4 The porter is carrying ....

5 The sailor is on the dock ....

(A) find their cabin on B Deck.

(B) loading goods onto the ship.

(C) is validating the ticket.

(D) in the cockpit before takeoff.

(E) the passengers' luggage through the station.

Strategy B

Be aware of similar sounds. The TOEIC® test often uses similar sounding words to confuse you. Note the similar sounding words in these examples.

(A) The train is in the station.
(B) The pants are on the hanger.
(C) The plane is in the hangar.
(D) The playing lane is narrow.

The correct answer is (C).

(A) They're being weighed today.
(B) They're waiting for a train.
(C) They're walking in the rain.
(D) They're loading grain.

The correct answer is (B).

Task B 📼

Identify the correct word

Listen to the pairs of sentences. Mark *1* beside the word you hear in the first sentence, and *2* beside the word you hear in the second sentence.

6 purse ....
   purser ....

7 musicians ....
   magicians ....

8 cars ....
   carts ....

9 thanked her ....
   tanker ....

10 let her ....
   letter ....

Review

Directions: Listen to the statements and choose the one that best describes what you see in the picture.

11

12

13

14

Listening Comprehension

Part I				
11	Ⓐ	Ⓑ	Ⓒ	Ⓓ
12	Ⓐ	Ⓑ	Ⓒ	Ⓓ
13	Ⓐ	Ⓑ	Ⓒ	Ⓓ
14	Ⓐ	Ⓑ	Ⓒ	Ⓓ

PART II

Strategy A

Listen for questions beginning with *what time*, *when* and *how* (*often*) for indications of time.

What time does the train depart?
When will the plane arrive?
How long does it take to get from here to your office?
How frequently does the express train run?
How often are there non-stop flights?
How much time do I need to get to the airport?
How soon will lunch be served?

Task A

Identify time

Underline the words that indicate time in the questions. Cross out the answer choice that is NOT possible.

1   <u>How frequently</u> does the freighter call at this port?
   (A)   About six times a year.
   (B)   ~~Any day now.~~
   (C)   Only twice a month.

2   When will the cabin attendants clean the cabin?
   (A)   They usually do it right after breakfast.
   (B)   When they are old enough.
   (C)   Whenever you want.

3   What time does the gate agent expect the flight to depart?
   (A)   At 5:15.
   (B)   As soon as the flight crew boards.
   (C)   On daylight saving time.

4   How many minutes more until we land?
   (A)   About ten.
   (B)   There are sixty in an hour.
   (C)   We should be on the ground in a few minutes.

5   How late do you expect the train to be?
   (A)   Earlier.
   (B)   Only a few minutes behind schedule.
   (C)   It won't be here for another hour at least.

6   How long will we have to wait for a taxi?
   (A)   In this rain, forever.
   (B)   More than a few minutes.
   (C)   I waited an hour for you.

7   On what days are there direct flights to Rio?
   (A)   Everyday but Monday.
   (B)   Any day now.
   (C)   Only on Wednesdays.

8   When do you think the fares will increase?
   (A)   At the end of this quarter.
   (B)   I think it is very expensive.
   (C)   They usually raise the prices every June.

9   How much longer will it take them to fuel the plane?
   (A)   Just a few more minutes.
   (B)   They should finish in a half an hour.
   (C)   It's a long time to go without fuel.

10   How often do passenger ships dock here?
   (A)   They rarely come here anymore.
   (B)   You see them here daily.
   (C)   At 4 in the afternoon.

Real Spoken English
How soon till we land?
This is the common spoken form of *How soon is it until we land?*
What about taking an earlier train?
This is the common spoken form of *Why don't we take a train that leaves earlier?*

Listen for time markers in *yes/no* questions.
A time marker is any word that helps you determine when an action occurs.

The plane is *always* on time, isn't it?
Can you tell me *when* the movie *begins*?
Do you think that the flight will be *late*?
Have the other flights been canceled *yet*?
You were supposed to *leave a week ago*, weren't you?
Is it possible to *finish* this *today*?
Your cruise took *longer* than you thought, didn't it?
I suppose they'll serve *dinner* on your flight, won't they?

Task B

Identify time markers in *yes / no* questions

Cross out the answer choice that is NOT possible. Then underline the time markers in the two possible answer choices.

11 Could you tell me when dinner is served?

(A) In about <u>five minutes</u>.
(B) ~~In the main dining room.~~
(C) At <u>7 p.m.</u>

12 Freighters are often behind schedule, aren't they?

(A) Yes, there are always delays on the trips.
(B) No, the schedule is in the front of the book.
(C) Yes, and a delay of one day is very costly.

13 If you don't leave soon, you'll miss your plane, won't you?

(A) I didn't realize how much I missed them.
(B) We need to leave now to get there on time.
(C) No, I allowed plenty of time.

14 Do you think they'll serve breakfast before landing?

(A) Yes, at 7 in the morning, about an hour before we touch down.
(B) I just have coffee for breakfast.
(C) No. Since we don't get in until noon, I think they'll serve lunch.

15 Wouldn't it be quicker to take the 8:15 train?

(A) It would be, but the 9:00 has a dining car.
(B) Yes, the early morning express is always faster.
(C) I tried to be quick, but I missed the train.

Review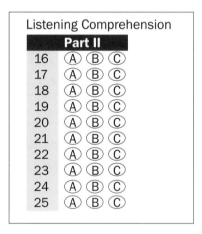

Directions: Listen and choose the best response to each question.

Listening Comprehension		
Part II		
16	Ⓐ Ⓑ Ⓒ	
17	Ⓐ Ⓑ Ⓒ	
18	Ⓐ Ⓑ Ⓒ	
19	Ⓐ Ⓑ Ⓒ	
20	Ⓐ Ⓑ Ⓒ	
21	Ⓐ Ⓑ Ⓒ	
22	Ⓐ Ⓑ Ⓒ	
23	Ⓐ Ⓑ Ⓒ	
24	Ⓐ Ⓑ Ⓒ	
25	Ⓐ Ⓑ Ⓒ	

PART III

Strategy A

Use the questions and answers to guess the topic of conversation. Look for questions that begin with *what*.

What is the problem?
What is the conversation about?
What are they discussing?

Task A

Identify the topic of conversation

Match the parts of the conversation to the appropriate answer choices.

1   What is the problem?

  (A)   Mr. Park's ticket is missing.
  (B)   Mr. Park is late for his flight.
  (C)   The road to the airport is closed.
  (D)   The taxi hasn't arrived.

I can't seem to remember where I put my ticket. ...*A*......
The cab should have been here ten minutes ago. ....
The traffic report said it was impossible to drive to the airport. ....
If I don't get to the gate in two minutes, they'll close the door. ....

> **Test Note**
> *What is the problem?* is a very common question on Part III of the TOEIC test.

2   What is the conversation about?

  (A)   A late departure.
  (B)   A sick crew member.
  (C)   A turbulent ride.
  (D)   A missed connection.

Our flight was canceled because one of the flight attendants became ill. ....
I only had ten minutes to get from one gate to the next, and by the time I got there, they had closed the door. ....
The captain requests that you remain in your seat with your seatbelts fastened. ....
Because of the weather, our flight will not leave as scheduled. ....

3   What are they discussing?

  (A)   Mechanical failure.
  (B)   A shortage of technicians.
  (C)   A potential strike.
  (D)   Worker benefits.

If the union demands aren't met, they will stop work. ....
It is difficult to find skilled and experienced workers to repair the electrical components in these cars. ....
All trains are delayed because of a problem with several engines. ....
The union employees gained increased health care and vacation days with the last contract. ....

4   What is the topic of discussion?

  (A)   Trains being late.
  (B)   A prerequisite for departure.
  (C)   An airport arrival.
  (D)   The use of public transportation.

He's probably coming on the next flight. ....
Snow on the tracks is the number one reason for delays in winter. ....
Mass transit in this city serves about 20% of commuters on a regular basis. ....
The ship can't sail until the engineer has arrived. ....

5   What is the problem?

  (A)   The bus is crowded.
  (B)   The passenger missed her stop.
  (C)   The driver couldn't make change.
  (D)   The rain was coming in the windows.

I'm sorry. You need the exact change on this bus. ....
Move to the rear of the bus. Make room for boarding passengers. ....
Driver! Driver! Stop the bus! Stop! I was supposed to get off. ....
Shut the windows! The seats will get wet. ....

Strategy B

Use the questions and answer choices to limit the possible reasons for an action. Pay attention to questions that begin with *why*.

Why is the hotel guest complaining?
Why has the tourist not unpacked her bags?
Why did the president not make the plane?

Task B

Identify the reason for an action

Read a line from a conversation. Then underline the answer choice that correctly identifies the reason.

6   "Marcia should take a book to read since the flight is long."
   Why should she take a book along?
   (A)   To pass the time.
   (B)   Because it's a best-seller.
   (C)   To make people think she is intelligent.
   (D)   She needs to write a book report.

7   "Mr. Sim is taking the train to Rome because he doesn't like to fly."
   Why is Mr. Sim taking the train?
   (A)   He enjoys watching the Italian scenery.
   (B)   The journey to Rome is too short to fly.
   (C)   He prefers not to fly.
   (D)   The plane was overbooked.

8   "Since I may not like the room, don't bring the bags until I check it out."
   Why doesn't the speaker want the bags brought to the room now?
   (A)   He's going to check out of the hotel.
   (B)   He wants to look the room over first.
   (C)   He wants to carry them himself.
   (D)   He's going to put them in storage.

9   "The constant motion of a ship makes me ill, so I've never taken a cruise."
   Why doesn't the speaker take a cruise?
   (A)   He doesn't like the constant activity.
   (B)   He has been in the hospital.
   (C)   He gets seasick.
   (D)   He can't afford it.

Review

Directions: Listen and choose the best answer to each question.

10   What is the problem?
   (A)   The plane is late.
   (B)   There are a lot of people in line.
   (C)   The man missed his flight.
   (D)   There are too many ticket agents.

11   Why can't the woman check in to her room?
   (A)   It's only 3 o'clock.
   (B)   The room is being made up now.
   (C)   Check-in time is at 12 o'clock.
   (D)   She doesn't have a reservation.

12   Why are they taking the train?
   (A)   It's more convenient.
   (B)   Their car is being repaired.
   (C)   They read an advertisement.
   (D)   They missed their flight.

13   What are they discussing?
   (A)   A romantic novel.
   (B)   Pleasures of ocean travel.
   (C)   Early explorations.
   (D)   Stormy weather.

Listening Comprehension			
Part III			
10	Ⓐ Ⓑ Ⓒ Ⓓ		
11	Ⓐ Ⓑ Ⓒ Ⓓ		
12	Ⓐ Ⓑ Ⓒ Ⓓ		
13	Ⓐ Ⓑ Ⓒ Ⓓ		

PART IV

Strategy A

Use the questions and answers to focus on the speaker and the audience of the talks. Look for questions that begin with *who*.

Who is talking?
Who is listening to this report?

As you listen to the talk, listen for people markers.

People Markers
Occupational titles:	*Dr, Captain*
Proper names:	*Mr, Mrs, Ms, Jack, Smith*
Collective nouns:	*the team, the crew*
Descriptive nouns:	*frequent flyers, people using this park*

Task A

Identify speaker and target listeners

Listen to three talks. Before each talk begins, read the answer choices quickly. Then choose the best answer.

1 Who is talking?

   (A) A pilot.
   (B) A flight attendant.
   (C) A gate agent.
   (D) A first class passenger.

2 To whom is the speaker talking?

   (A) Only frequent flyers.
   (B) The cabin crew.
   (C) The ground staff.
   (D) All passengers.

3 Who is talking?

   (A) A purser.
   (B) A travel agent.
   (C) A sailor.
   (D) A social director.

4 To whom is the speaker talking?

   (A) Potential travelers.
   (B) Novice sailors.
   (C) Musicians.
   (D) Hotel staff.

5 Who is most likely talking?

   (A) A tour guide.
   (B) A shopper from New York.
   (C) A shopkeeper.
   (D) A citizen of New Jersey.

6 To whom is the speaker talking?

   (A) Tourists.
   (B) Actresses.
   (C) Luxury store owners.
   (D) Tour guides.

Strategy B

Use the questions and answers to focus on numbers in quantities, times, and amounts. Before the talks begin, read the questions and the answer choices quickly. Pay attention to questions that begin with *when* and *how*.

When did he arrive?
When was the timetable published?
How long will the flight last?
How much does the ticket cost?

Task B

Identify quantity and amount

Cross out the sentence that does NOT have the same meaning as the other two.

7   We need at least a dozen towels.
    I asked for a couple of towels.
    Don't give us less than twelve.

8   She'll be staying at the hotel for two weeks.
    Her reservation is for fourteen days.
    She'll check out in five-business days.

9   I need this in less than 24 hours – no later than noon.
    Is it possible to have it ready by 12:00 tomorrow?
    Anytime after dinner is fine.

10 All of the tickets cost $10.
    He bought ten tickets which cost $100 each.
    He spent $1000 on tickets.

Review 📼

Directions: Listen and choose the best answer to each question.

11   Who is speaking?
     (A) An army captain.
     (B) An airline captain.
     (C) A sea captain.
     (D) A restaurant captain.

12   When will the plane land?
     (A) In 10 minutes.
     (B) In 20 minutes.
     (C) In 30 minutes.
     (D) In 70 minutes.

13   What was the average hotel occupancy rate?
     (A) 40%.
     (B) 60%.
     (C) 80%.
     (D) 100%.

14   Who is making the toast?
     (A) A hotel guest.
     (B) A hotel manager.
     (C) A room clerk.
     (D) A travel agent.

Listening Comprehension			
Part IV			
11	Ⓐ Ⓑ Ⓒ Ⓓ		
12	Ⓐ Ⓑ Ⓒ Ⓓ		
13	Ⓐ Ⓑ Ⓒ Ⓓ		
14	Ⓐ Ⓑ Ⓒ Ⓓ		

Reading PART V

Strategy A

Look at the words around the blank and focus on their grammatical forms to determine the missing part of speech.

When the price of oil rises, the price of air tickets ....
- (A)   increases
- (B)   increased
- (C)   increasing
- (D)   increasingly

When	the	price	of	oil	rises,	the	price	of	air tickets	....
conj.	det.	noun	prep	noun	verb	det.	noun	prep	noun	verb

Choice (A) *increases* can be a noun or verb.
Choice (B) *increased* can be a verb or a participle.
Choice (C) *increasing* is a participle.
Choice (D) *increasingly* is an adverb.

The correct answer is (A). The main clause needs a verb. Answer choices (A) and (B) are both verbs. The verb in the sub clause is in the present simple tense and talks generally about when things happen. The main clause should also be in this tense, so the correct answer is (A).

> **Grammar Glossary** Parts of Speech (p217)   **Word Families** (p221)

Task A

Identify the part of speech

**Write the part of speech (noun, verb, adverb, adjective) for each answer choice.
Then choose the word or phrase that best completes the sentence.**

1   The .... of many countries depends on tourism.
- (A)   economize ....
- (B)   economical ....
- (C)   economically ....
- (D)   economy ....

2   The hotel director .... a large staff.
- (A)   management ....
- (B)   manager ....
- (C)   manages ....
- (D)   managerial ....

3   When .... airlines are privatized, service usually improves.
- (A)   national ....
- (B)   nation ....
- (C)   nationality ....
- (D)   nationalize ....

4   If you express yourself .... , it will be easier for people to understand you.
- (A)   simple ....
- (B)   simplification ....
- (C)   simplify ....
- (D)   simply ....

5   Museums are visited more often by tourists than ....
- (A)   location ....
- (B)   locate ....
- (C)   locals ....
- (D)   localize ....

6   Package .... are extremely popular with elderly and single travelers.
- (A)   tourism ....
- (B)   toured ....
- (C)   tourists ....
- (D)   tours ....

Strategy B

Look for passive verb markers to complete a prepositional phrase.
An active verb is changed into a passive one by changing the active verb into
the past participle form and putting a form of the verb *to be* in front of it.
The preposition *by* usually follows. These are both indications that the verb is
a passive verb.

> Active: An experienced guide gave the tour.
> Passive: The tour *was given by* an experienced guide.

Grammar Glossary **Verbs: Active/Passive**   (p219)

Task B

Identify the appropriate preposition

Underline the correct preposition. Then mark *P* if the verb is passive or *A* if it is active.

7   The brochure was written *by / to* an experienced travel agent. ....

8   The translator wrote *by / to* the editor. ....

9   The room was cleaned *by / upon* the head housekeeper. ....

10   The maintenance crew cleaned the aircraft *by / upon* arrival. ....

11   The train doesn't stop *by / at* every station during rush hour. ....

Review

Directions: Choose the one word that best completes the sentence.

12   Airline policies ……….. the amount of carry-on luggage.

   (A) limit
   (B) limitation
   (C) limitless
   (D) limiting

13   This ticket needs to be endorsed ……….. the issuing agent.

   (A) on
   (B) with
   (C) by
   (D) at

14   The flight attendant gave a safety ……….. before take off.

   (A) demonstrator
   (B) demonstration
   (C) demonstrate
   (D) demonstrable

15   Large bags must be checked ……….. airline personnel.

   (A) from
   (B) to
   (C) toward
   (D) by

16   The tour guide ……….. the sites she would show us.

   (A) described
   (B) description
   (C) describable
   (D) describing

Reading			
Part V			
12	Ⓐ Ⓑ Ⓒ Ⓓ		
13	Ⓐ Ⓑ Ⓒ Ⓓ		
14	Ⓐ Ⓑ Ⓒ Ⓓ		
15	Ⓐ Ⓑ Ⓒ Ⓓ		
16	Ⓐ Ⓑ Ⓒ Ⓓ		

PART VI

Strategy A

When you see a pronoun underlined in this section of the TOEIC test, check that it isn't a second subject. A pronoun is often added to a sentence to make the subject redundant.

Travel agents <u>hope</u> the cold weather <u>it</u> will increase sales <u>of</u> package tours to <u>tropical</u> countries.
　　　　　　　 A　　　　　　　　　　　 B　　　　　　　　　 C　　　　　　　　 D

There are two clauses in this sentence.
Main clause: Travel agents hope [+noun clause]
Noun clause: (that) the cold weather will increase sales.

The subject of the noun clause is *weather*, the verb is *increase*. A clause needs only one subject. *It* was added to distract you. Therefore, (B) is incorrect.

> **Grammar glossary** **Clauses: Main and Subordinate Clauses** (p214)
> **Subject: Redundant Subject** (p219)

Task A

Identify the subject of a sentence

Mark *MC* above the main clause and *SC* above the subordinate clause.
Then underline the subjects in each clause.

1　　　　　　　　　　　　　　　 *SC*　　　　　　　　　　　　　　　　　　　 *MC*
　When <u>you</u> cross the Pacific in our business class, our <u>spacious seating</u> gives you more room to stretch out.

2　With our wide network of car rental locations, you can drop off your car at any location.

3　Once first class fares are lowered, demand for first class will increase.

4　Passenger trains, which share tracks with freight trains, are often late.

5　City regulations require that taxi cabs wait at designated locations.

Strategy B

Look out for the form of a verb separated from its subject.
On the TOEIC test many words, phrases, or clauses often separate the subject from its verb. Look carefully for the subject.

A <u>messenger</u> service comes to the <u>office</u>, picks up the tickets, and <u>deliver</u> them
   A   B   C
to your clients <u>every</u> morning.
                  D

The subject of the sentence is *service*, which is singular. The two verbs that follow immediately are third person singular: *comes*, *picks up*. The third verb *deliver* must be in the third person singular, too. Therefore, (C) *deliver* is incorrect.

Be careful when the verb is far from the subject. Also be careful when a noun close to the verb (in this case *tickets*) is plural, but is not its subject.

Grammar Glossary **Subject and Verbs of a Sentence** (p219)
Verb Agreement (p220)

Task B

Identify subject/verb agreement

Underline the subjects below and mark *S* for a singular subject, *NC* for non-count or *P* for plural. Write the correct form of the verb if it is incorrect.

6   ^S <u>A cruise</u> aboard the new *Titanic* or its sister ship

      Grand <s>are</s> *is* available at bargain prices now.

7   Seats on all of our flights, including the coach-only flight to Madrid, is assigned on the day of departure.

8   The itinerary given to all travelers was a four-city trip in five days.

9   The Travel Association's annual business travel forecast predict overall travel costs jumping 5% next year.

10   Once luggage are checked at the ticket counter, it is routed through a high-tech security scanner.

11   The hotel, one of the newest in the chain, is located a mile south of the airport and include a golf-course on the grounds.

12   Disembarking from the plane to a waiting bus is not as convenient as walking off the plane using a jet way.

13   The restaurants located on boats in the harbor and the new restaurant on the dock specializes in seafood.

14   Most of the city's major business hotels line avenues parallel to the beach.

15   Airlines, which compete to provide the best service, offers amenities like a personal video at every seat.

Review

Directions: Identify the one underlined word or phrase that should be corrected or rewritten.

16 Many airline companies, <u>which</u> use the Internet <u>to communicate</u> with customers
AB
<u>they</u> send <u>their</u> announcements by e-mail.
CD

17 The hotel <u>executive</u> director, having <u>supervised</u> a major renovation of the hotel, <u>she</u> left
ABC
<u>to manage</u> another property.
D

18 The express trains <u>which</u> arrive on the north platform <u>is</u> only in <u>the</u> station for one <u>minute</u>.
ABCD

19 A token, which <u>are</u> good on all subway <u>lines</u>, can be <u>purchased</u> from <u>vending</u> machines.
ABCD

20 The taxi meter, which is <u>supplied</u> by a <u>leasing</u> company, <u>it</u> must be installed by a certified <u>technician</u>.
ABCD

21 Hiring a car <u>and</u> driver to get to appointments <u>are</u> increasingly <u>a</u> necessity rather than a <u>luxury</u>.
ABCD

22 A hotel's concierge, trained never to say the word "impossible," <u>he</u> is skilled at <u>getting</u> you
AB
<u>whatever</u> you <u>need</u>.
CD

23 The airline <u>mechanics</u>, <u>who</u> <u>maintains</u> the company's large fleet of 747s, <u>are</u> on strike.
ABCD

24 <u>Complimentary</u> chauffeur service is provided <u>for</u> any guest who <u>have</u> business with our <u>company</u>.
ABCD

25 The trolley, <u>used</u> to transport luggage <u>through</u> the airport, <u>are</u> usually left <u>outside</u>.
ABCD

Reading

	Part VI		
16 Ⓐ Ⓑ Ⓒ Ⓓ		21 Ⓐ Ⓑ Ⓒ Ⓓ	
17 Ⓐ Ⓑ Ⓒ Ⓓ		22 Ⓐ Ⓑ Ⓒ Ⓓ	
18 Ⓐ Ⓑ Ⓒ Ⓓ		23 Ⓐ Ⓑ Ⓒ Ⓓ	
19 Ⓐ Ⓑ Ⓒ Ⓓ		24 Ⓐ Ⓑ Ⓒ Ⓓ	
20 Ⓐ Ⓑ Ⓒ Ⓓ		25 Ⓐ Ⓑ Ⓒ Ⓓ	

PART VII

Strategy A

Use the question and answers to focus on restrictions.
Read the questions and answer choices before you read the passage.
Learn to look for what is NOT stated.

> What type of clothing may NOT be worn in the lobby?
> (A) Swim attire
> (B) Golf shoes
> (C) Running outfits
> (D) Bathrobes

Notice

Our guests are kindly requested not to run in the pool area or to wear golf shoes on the rubber mat surrounding the pool. We ask that guests crossing the lobby from the swimming pool wear cover-up garments like a bathrobe.

(A) is the correct answer.

In the question above there are keywords that answer *what* and *where*. *What* is the *type of clothing* and *where* is *the lobby*. Your task is to identify the article of clothing that can NOT be worn in the lobby.

Read the notice quickly and look for the four answer choices. The verb *run* and the noun phrase *golf shoes* are found, but they are associated with the pool area not the lobby. So you can eliminate (B) and (C). Only (A) *swim attire* (swim suits) and (D) *bathrobes* are associated with the lobby. A quick reading indicates that hotel guests should conceal their swimsuits, that is they should hide them and NOT let them be seen in the lobby. Therefore (D) is not the correct answer as bathrobes are allowed to be worn in the lobby. This leaves (A).

Task A

Identify restrictions

Cross out the answer choices that are NOT related to the main underlined topic.

1   <u>Patio furniture</u> is NOT to be removed.
   (A)   ~~Trees~~
   (B)   Chairs
   (C)   Seat cushions
   (D)   ~~Medicine cabinets~~

2   In case of <u>emergency</u>, locate the exit nearest you.
   (A)   Earthquake
   (B)   Fire
   (C)   Fatigue
   (D)   Flooding

3   <u>Disabled passengers or passengers needing special accommodation</u> are invited to board at this time.
   (A)   Passengers in wheelchairs
   (B)   Passengers with first-class tickets
   (C)   Elderly passengers
   (D)   Passengers with small children

4   <u>Change is NOT given without purchase.</u>
   (A)   I can only get small coins if I buy something.
   (B)   I can only use small coins to buy something.
   (C)   When I buy something, I can get some single bills or coins.
   (D)   I cannot exchange anything I buy.

Strategy B

Read the answer choices and text quickly to look for time markers.
As you learn to look for specific answers to specific questions, you will learn to avoid irrelevant information.

At what time of day are there the most flights?
(A)   Early in the morning
(B)   At noon
(C)   Mid-afternoon
(D)   Late evening

Flight Schedule from Antwerp		
0600	AF3200	Paris
0600	SQ 1	Singapore
0610	KG 342	Frankfurt
0630	LH 452	Strutgart
0635	BA 818	London
1215	AF 1627	Lille
1230	LH 334	Berlin
1315	BA 819	London
1530	AF 1440	Paris
1540	TY 234	Istanbul
1850	BA 820	London
2000	LH 56	Munich

(A) is the correct answer. The key words *what time* indicate that you are to locate *when*. The key words *most flights* tell you *what*.

Before you read the passage, you should quickly translate the answer choices into time blocks.

Choice (A) *Early in the morning* is between 5:00 a.m. and 9:00 a.m. approximately.

Choice (B) *At noon* is around twelve o'clock.

Choice (C) *Mid-afternoon* is between 2:30 p.m. and 4:00 p.m.

Choice (D) *Late evening* is after 10:00 p.m.

A quick scan of the schedule shows that the most flights leave between 0600 and 0635 in fact almost 50% of the flights leave at that time. Therefore, the correct answer is (A), *Early in the morning*.

Task B

Identify time

Match the time markers (A–F) with their approximate equivalents (5–10).

5	in a week	(A)	daily
6	biannually	(B)	twice a year
7	every two weeks	(C)	in two days' time
8	every day	(D)	within seven days
9	an hour and a half	(E)	90 minutes
10	the day after tomorrow	(F)	fortnightly

Review

Directions: Read the information and choose the one best answer (A), (B), (C) or (D) to each question.

Questions 11–14 refer to the following information.

> To ensure that your reservation on China Air is not canceled, you must check-in for all domestic flights one hour before boarding time. You must be at the departure gate twenty minutes before boarding time. For international flights, you must check in at least two hours before boarding time. You must be at the departure gate thirty minutes before boarding time.
>
> Travelers to Hong Kong or Macao must check in 90 minutes before boarding time.
>
> All international travelers are required to reconfirm their flight at least 72 hours prior to departure. Flights to Hong Kong or Macao do not require reconfirmation.

11 When must domestic travelers report to the departure gate?
- (A) Immediately after checking in
- (B) 20 minutes before boarding
- (C) A half hour before boarding
- (D) Before checking in

12 Travelers to Macao do NOT have to do which of the following?
- (A) Check in
- (B) Be at the departure gate prior to departure
- (C) Reconfirm their reservations
- (D) Check in one and one-half hours before boarding time

13 How many minutes before departure should international travelers check-in?
- (A) 20
- (B) 30
- (C) 90
- (D) 120

14 Which travelers must confirm three days in advance to ensure their reservations?
- (A) International travelers
- (B) Domestic travelers
- (C) Travelers to Macao or Hong Kong
- (D) All travelers follow the same procedure

Reading

Part VII				
11	Ⓐ	Ⓑ	Ⓒ	Ⓓ
12	Ⓐ	Ⓑ	Ⓒ	Ⓓ
13	Ⓐ	Ⓑ	Ⓒ	Ⓓ
14	Ⓐ	Ⓑ	Ⓒ	Ⓓ

Listening comprehension PART I

Strategy A

Use the pictures to determine specific details. The TOEIC® test often uses statements that seem to be correct. These statements describe the picture generally, but yet are wrong about a specific detail. Ask yourself *where* to determine the general context and the specific context.

General Context
The man is in the control room.

Specific Details
The engineer is looking at the controls on the right.
The chair is on wheels.

General Context
The woman is in the laboratory.

Specific Details
The technician is looking through the microscope.
There are flasks and bottles in front of the woman.

Task A

Identify the specific details

Write the letters of two specific details that match the general context.

General Context

1   The computer is in a room.   *A*   *F*

2   The people are in the studio.   ....

3   He's standing by the machine.   ....

4   The drawings are on the wall.   ....

5   She's pouring liquid.   ....

Specific Details
(A) The laptop computer is in the manager's office.
(B) The diagrams are taped to the wall.
(C) A man is unpacking the fax machine.
(D) The sound technicians are checking the microphones.
(E) The researcher is adding liquid to a beaker.
(F) The computer's monitor is on a shelf.
(G) The musicians are getting ready to record.
(H) The office technician is opening a box.
(I) The laboratory assistant is holding a beaker.
(J) They are diagrams of electrical circuit boards.

Strategy B

Be aware of homophones and homonyms.
The TOEIC test often uses words that sound the same but have different meanings. This is done to distract you from the correct answer. Look at these words in these examples.

(A)   The crane's lifting a steel <u>bar</u>.
(B)   They're working in a <u>bar</u>.

The correct answer is (A).

(A)   The windmills are on the <u>plain</u>.
(B)   The propellers are on the <u>plane</u>.

The correct answer is (A).

Task B

Identify the similar sounding words

Read sentence 6, then listen to two sentences. Mark _A_ or _B_ to indicate the sentence that is related to the sentence you read. Listen again and write the homophone or homonym that you hear in each of the two sentences. Continue with sentences 7–10.

	_A / B_	_homophone / homonym_
6	....B.... The motor made an unusual noise when we turned it on.	.............belt..............
7	.... The computer room was filled with the new trainees.	....
8	.... Over fifty microscopes were installed in the laboratory.	....
9	.... When we moved the ladder, we knocked over the toolbox.	....
10	.... All of the wires from the appliances created a fire hazard.	....

Review 📼

Directions: Listen to the statements and choose the one that best describes what you see in the picture.

11

12

13

14

Listening Comprehension				
Part I				
11	Ⓐ	Ⓑ	Ⓒ	Ⓓ
12	Ⓐ	Ⓑ	Ⓒ	Ⓓ
13	Ⓐ	Ⓑ	Ⓒ	Ⓓ
14	Ⓐ	Ⓑ	Ⓒ	Ⓓ

PART II

Strategy A

Listen for question words that ask for a reason. Questions that ask for a reason usually begin with *why*. The reason itself may begin with *because*, or a reason may be stated without the need of *because*.

> Why did you buy that type of calculator?
> *Because* it can perform a number of functions.

> Why didn't you attend the neuroscience conference?
> I was in the middle of some experiments and I didn't have the time.

Task A

Identify the possible reason

Cross out the answer choices that are NOT possible.

1   Why did you buy new appliances?
   (A) At the store on the corner near the school and the hospital.
   (B) They use a different voltage system.
   (C) I don't think the old ones will work in Brazil.

2   Why are the utility crews in the intersection?
   (A) The men in the orange jackets.
   (B) They're doing an annual inspection.
   (C) One of the water mains broke.

3   Why does it take so long to fuel the airplane?
   (A) Jets use so much fuel that it has to be stored in the wings.
   (B) Because the tanks are already full.
   (C) Fuel is added slowly and carefully.

4   Why did they take the machine apart?
   (A) The tools are right there.
   (B) Someone spilled coffee on it.
   (C) There seemed to be a short in the connections.

5   Why does the company continue to use Good Earth's landscaping?
   (A) We couldn't have made a smarter move.
   (B) Their rates are more competitive.
   (C) The owner is a friend of the president.

6   Why did the new engineer disassemble all of the machines?
   (A) To find the defective parts.
   (B) It was the fifth time the machines were returned.
   (C) It was the only way to solve the problem.

7   Why is the research and development office closing?
   (A) An article about their research was published recently.
   (B) They've added more staff.
   (C) R & D is no longer being funded.

8   Why are they reducing the technical service staff?
   (A) The volume of calls has dropped dramatically in the last year.
   (B) The company has contracted with an outside company to handle the problems.
   (C) I don't care how long I have to wait if they can fix it.

9   Why haven't they released the latest version of the computer operating system?
   (A) The computer has many new programs installed.
   (B) They wanted to wait until they could fix the bugs.
   (C) No, they haven't been on display.

10 Why are all of the containers still on the dock?
   (A) The workers went on strike last night.
   (B) There was an electrical malfunction with the cranes.
   (C) There are over 50 shipments from China sitting on the deck.

Strategy B

To identify opinion questions, add "*What do you think?*" Then listen for answer choices that show what the speaker thinks.

> *Should we hire the recent college graduate?*

You can easily add "What do you think, should we hire the college graduate?" and identify that the question is asking for an opinion. The answer choice should indicate an opinion, not a fact.

Real Spoken English
In common speech, we often voice our opinions by starting with:

In my opinion …
or
I think …
or
I believe that …

In the TOEIC test, these clues are often omitted.

Task B

Identify the possible opinion

Cross out the answer choice that is NOT possible.

11 Can we finish the installation today?
    (A) They close in fifteen minutes.
    (B) If we hurry, we should be able to.
    (C) It's going to be difficult.

12 Will the current system be adequate for our energy needs in 10 years?
    (A) We hope that it will be.
    (B) Five years ago we changed systems.
    (C) The experts don't believe that it will be.

13 What are the results of the experiment?
    (A) We received them around an hour ago.
    (B) They turned out surprisingly well.
    (C) We're divided on how we should interpret them.

14 What do you think of the physical plant?
    (A) It has seen better days.
    (B) The boiler rooms need some upkeep.
    (C) Because it is old and inefficient.

15 Have we ordered enough cables?
    (A) Jack did his best to accurately predict the amount needed.
    (B) Definitely.
    (C) No, we didn't use any.

Review

Directions: Listen and choose the best response to each question.

Listening Comprehension
Part II
16 Ⓐ Ⓑ Ⓒ
17 Ⓐ Ⓑ Ⓒ
18 Ⓐ Ⓑ Ⓒ
19 Ⓐ Ⓑ Ⓒ
20 Ⓐ Ⓑ Ⓒ
21 Ⓐ Ⓑ Ⓒ
22 Ⓐ Ⓑ Ⓒ
23 Ⓐ Ⓑ Ⓒ
24 Ⓐ Ⓑ Ⓒ
25 Ⓐ Ⓑ Ⓒ

PART III

Use the questions and answers to identify a time. Look for question words like *when* that ask for a time. You usually see a preposition in front of the time.

When will you be done?
(A)   <u>In</u> a short while.
(B)   <u>By</u> the time you get here.
(C)   <u>At</u> ten o'clock.
(D)   <u>In</u> around fifteen minutes.

> **Grammar Glossary** **Prepositional Phrases with *by*** (p218)

Task A

Identify a time

Underline the prepositions. Then check the answer choices that answer the question *when*.

1   (A)   By the end of the month.
    (B)   They started eight weeks ago.
    (C)   Hopefully in a couple of weeks.
    (D)   The inspection is in two weeks.

2   (A)   She finished her degree last year.
    (B)   At the end of last fall.
    (C)   Right after she finished her graduate program.
    (D)   Her first job was in Boston.

3   (A)   They consider it a good investment.
    (B)   As soon as the system's errors were fixed.
    (C)   It is an immense improvement over the last project.
    (D)   The prices came down on the day we arrived.

4   (A)   It is due to open in a month.
    (B)   During the last government's term.
    (C)   It is on the border of Argentina and Brazil.
    (D)   In 1988.

5   (A)   The week after next.
    (B)   To make sure we have the fastest equipment.
    (C)   After the regional meetings.
    (D)   The CEO comes from a different industry.

Strategy B

Look for questions that ask to identify an occupation. Read the answer choices quickly. Then ask yourself the questions below about each of the occupations.

(A)   Engineer.
(B)   Doctor.
(C)   Plumber.
(D)   Carpet Installer.

Where does he or she work?
What does he or she do?
What kind of equipment does he or she use?

Task B

Identify the correct occupation

Listen to the conversations. Cross out the answer choices that are NOT possible.

6   What is the man's occupation?

    (A) Automechanic.
    (B) Pilot.
    (C) Plumber.
    (D) Carpet installer.

7   Who are the speakers?

    (A) Nurses.
    (B) Patients.
    (C) Doctors.
    (D) Construction workers.

8   What does the man do?

    (A) He's an air conditioning specialist.
    (B) He's a computer programmer.
    (C) He's a graphic designer.
    (D) He's a pest control expert.

9   What is the woman's job?

    (A) A TV presenter.
    (B) A service representative.
    (C) A customer service representative.
    (D) A telephone installer.

Review

Directions: Listen and choose the best answer to each question.

10   What is probably their occupation?

    (A) Scientist.
    (B) Eye doctor.
    (C) Repair technician.
    (D) Flight controller.

11   What does the woman do?

    (A) She's a counsellor.
    (B) She's a mail carrier.
    (C) She's a telephone operator.
    (D) She's a computer specialist.

12   By when does the man need the cellular phones?

    (A) The date is not important.
    (B) Before the union meeting.
    (C) Before May 1.
    (D) Before the factory opens.

13   How long have they been waiting for the information?

    (A) One day.
    (B) Five weeks.
    (C) Two months.
    (D) Three months.

Listening Comprehension			
Part III			
10	Ⓐ	Ⓑ	Ⓒ Ⓓ
11	Ⓐ	Ⓑ	Ⓒ Ⓓ
12	Ⓐ	Ⓑ	Ⓒ Ⓓ
13	Ⓐ	Ⓑ	Ⓒ Ⓓ

PART IV

Strategy A

Use the questions and answer choices to focus on the emotions and opinions of the talk. Look for questions that begin with *how* and *what*.

> *How* do the workers feel?
> *How* will the engineer react?
> *What* is the tone of the talk?

Answer choices to the questions above will include adjectives describing the people and the tone.

Task A

Identify the tone

Listen to three talks. Before each talk begins, read the answer choices quickly. Then choose the best answer.

1   How do the trainees feel?

  (A) Incompetent.
  (B) Nervous.
  (C) Excited.
  (D) Bored.

2   How does ACME regard its trainees?

  (A) With pride.
  (B) With suspicion.
  (C) With alarm.
  (D) With distrust.

3   What is the speaker's mood?

  (A) Angry.
  (B) Relaxed.
  (C) Serious.
  (D) Hesitant.

4   How will the speaker react if anyone asks a question?

  (A) Happily.
  (B) Friendly.
  (C) Calmly.
  (D) Impatiently.

5   What kind of person is being addressed?

  (A) A concerned business person.
  (B) A disinterested worker.
  (C) An energetic banker.
  (D) An indifferent consumer.

6   How does the announcer want the listener to feel?

  (A) Interested.
  (B) Frightened.
  (C) Anxious.
  (D) Depressed.

Strategy B

Use the questions and answers to identify the point of view.
A *point of view* is an opinion or a way of looking at something.

> *What* does the speaker think?
> *What* is the speaker's point of view?
> *What* is the audience's point of view?

Task B

Identify points of view

Cross out the sentences that do NOT express a point of view.

7 (A) She is difficult to work with.
   (B) She has a ticket for the next train.
   (C) She often disagrees with her colleagues.
   (D) I think she is very opinionated.

8 (A) We have been voted the world's leader in engineering supplies for three years in a row.
   (B) They should be the leader in engineering supplies.
   (C) If they continue along the same path, the company will be the leader in engineering supplies.
   (D) In 1995, they sold more engineering supplies than any other company.

9 (A) The spare parts were ordered last week.
   (B) If we don't receive the spare parts, the assembly line may have to close.
   (C) The distributor of spare parts is very unreliable.
   (D) They determined that the skyrocketing price of parts caused five companies to go out of business.

10 (A) According to policy, any malfunctions are to be reported immediately.
   (B) I believe that the machine broke down due to overuse.
   (C) This is the fifth time that we've had to call for repairs on the machine.
   (D) The machine is in the back against the left hand wall.

Review

Directions: Listen and choose the best answer to each question.

11 What is the speaker's point of view?
    (A) The problem can be solved.
    (B) One person is to blame.
    (C) The early shift should stay late.
    (D) The workers should not leave.

12 What is the tone of the speaker?
    (A) Friendly.
    (B) Defensive.
    (C) Concerned.
    (D) Terrified.

13 According to the speaker, what is most important?
    (A) Customer reaction.
    (B) Worker satisfaction.
    (C) Cost cutting measures.
    (D) Suppliers' deadlines.

14 How does the speaker feel?
    (A) Unconcerned.
    (B) Realistic.
    (C) Desperate.
    (D) Infuriated.

Listening Comprehension			
Part IV			
11	Ⓐ Ⓑ Ⓒ Ⓓ		
12	Ⓐ Ⓑ Ⓒ Ⓓ		
13	Ⓐ Ⓑ Ⓒ Ⓓ		
14	Ⓐ Ⓑ Ⓒ Ⓓ		

Reading PART V

Grammar Glossary Nouns: Count/Non-count (p216)
Nouns: Singular/Plural (p216)

Task A

Identify count and non-count nouns

Underline the nouns that the verbs refer to. Mark *C* if they are count or *NC* if they are non-count. Then choose the correct form and tense of the verbs.

C
The scientists carefully (1) ....*D*..... the results of their research which (2) .....*C*.....
extremely valuable.

1	2
(A) guarding	(A) were
(B) guards	(B) has been
(C) are guarded	(C) are
(D) guard	(D) is

His advice, which (3) .... followed over the years, (4) .... allowed the company to succeed where many others have failed.

3	4
(A) is	(A) has
(B) were	(B) have
(C) are	(C) had
(D) was	(D) have been

Mathematics (5) .... one of the most demanding fields, yet (6) .... to draw some of the best and the brightest students.

5	6
(A) are	(A) continuing
(B) were	(B) continued
(C) am	(C) continue
(D) is	(D) continues

Strategy B

Read the sentence quickly to make sure that the meaning of the answer choice that you select is appropriate in the context of the sentence. Words that may mean the same in one context (synonyms) may not both be correct in a different context.

The foreman pulled the bell .... the end of the shift.
(A)   turning
(B)   lighting
(C)   signaling
(D)   intimating

The correct answer is (C), *signaling*. A bell cannot turn or light the end of a shift, so answer choices (A) and (B) are incorrect. Answer choice (D) looks and sounds similar to *indicate*, which is a synonym of signal, however intimate is incorrect.

Grammar Glossary **Synonyms** (p219)

Task B

Identify the synonyms

Cross out the words which are NOT synonyms of the underlined word.

7   The architects were making good progress and should be in the final planning <u>stage</u> by mid-week.

(A)   phase
(B)   curtain
(C)   wage
(D)   step

8   Technology has advanced at such a rapid <u>pace</u> that it is difficult for companies to remain current.

(A)   rate
(B)   tariff
(C)   rhythm
(D)   speed

9   The ground water had <u>seeped</u> into the pipes causing a substantial amount of damage.

(A)   sipped
(B)   entered
(C)   slipped
(D)   moved

10   Human error was a contributing <u>factor</u> to the power plant accident.

(A)   reason
(B)   information
(C)   cause
(D)   energy

11   Upon examining the circuits, they were able to identify the cause of electrical <u>malfunction</u>.

(A)   failure
(B)   negative
(C)   breakdown
(D)   efficient

Review

Directions: Choose the one word that best completes the sentence.

12 The most skilled technicians in the lab .... meeting now with the new trainees.

(A) were
(B) is
(C) was
(D) are

13 The manufacturers of the engine were unable to locate the .... part in order to fill the order.

(A) required
(B) obligation
(C) necessity
(D) retired

14 The equipment must be serviced on a .... basis, every two weeks, to maintain its efficiency.

(A) customary
(B) common
(C) regular
(D) usual

15 The sources of the information .... listed in the back of the manual.

(A) are
(B) isn't
(C) aren't
(D) is

16 The plumbers received an emergency call when the main .... broke suddenly.

(A) pipe
(B) jar
(C) metal
(D) barrel

Reading

	Part V			
12	(A)	(B)	(C)	(D)
13	(A)	(B)	(C)	(D)
14	(A)	(B)	(C)	(D)
15	(A)	(B)	(C)	(D)
16	(A)	(B)	(C)	(D)

PART VI

Strategy A

When you see sentences that begin with or contain the word *if*, ask yourself if they are conditional statements. Identify if the conditional sentence is a real or hypothetical situation. Then, check to see that the correct form of the verb is used.

> (A)   *If* the company *has* a large enough budget, it *will be able to expand* its market.
> (B)   *If* they *had* an unlimited budget, our plans *would look* very different.
> (C)   *If* the management *had added* more money to its advertising budget, we *could have reached* more markets.

In the examples above, all sentences begin with *if* and are conditional sentences. Sentence (A) relates to a potential *real* situation (real future possibility); Sentence (B) describes a *present hypothetical* situation (present unreal possibility); Sentence (C) describes a *past hypothetical* situation (past unreal possibility). Note the verb tenses in each sentence.

> Grammar Glossary **Conditionals** (p214)

Task A

Identify conditional sentences

Complete the sentences with the correct form of the verb. The sentences are identified as real or as present or past hypothetical.

1   If the city *identified* the source of the leaks, it (save) _would save_ the taxpayers millions of dollars. *Present hypothetical*

2   If I (know) .... that e-commerce was going to be such a financial success, I *would have invested* my money in different companies. *Past Hypothetical*

3   If the connection *is* made correctly the first time, there (be) .... no need to do any rewiring. *Real*

4   If management *values* savings and efficiency, they (contact) .... us about our newest software programs. *Real*

5   The farm machinery (not rust) .... if the family *had invested* in repairs to the barn. *Past Hypothetical*

Strategy B

Look out for adjectives that end in *-ed* (or other past participle ending, *-en*, *-t*, etc.) and *-ing*. Make sure that the form is correct for the meaning of the sentence.

The meaning might be **cause** (*-ing*) or **effect** (*-ed*).

> The investors heard some *frightening* news about the stock market.
> The *frightened* investors took their money out of the stock market.

Frightening describes the news, which causes the investors' feeling.
Frightened describes how the investors feel, which is the effect of the news.

Participle adjectives can also describe something that is **in progress** (*-ing*) or **completed** (*-ed*).

> Watch out for the *falling* bricks. (The bricks are falling.)
> The sidewalk was covered with *fallen* bricks. (The bricks fell down before and now they are lying on the sidewalk.)

Participle adjectives with *-ing* can describe a person or thing that is **active**.
> *Working* parents are very busy. (The parents work)
> The sound of *dripping* water helped us discover the leak. (The water drips)

Grammar Glossary **Participles: *-ed / -ing* (p217)**

Task B

Identify participle adjectives

Underline the correct form of the adjective.

6   Artificial intelligence is extremely *interested/interesting* to me.

7   These offices are chilly because the *heated/heating* system isn't working well.

8   The computer scientist tries not to make his lectures *complicated/complicating*, but he isn't usually successful.

9   The constant hum of the machinery was so *annoyed/annoying* that the employees had a hard time concentrating on their work.

10   The *tired/tiring* mechanic came to fix the machine at the end of the day.

11   The foreman was *puzzled/puzzling* by the miners' reluctance to return to work.

12   If you could teach me to fix these recurring problems, your job would be much more *relaxed/relaxing*.

13   They complain that the *painted/painting* body of the car is often chipped during shipping.

14   Entering the harbor by tugboat, the *loaded/loading* freighter finally reached its destination.

15   The *speeded/speeding* traffic makes this a dangerous street to cross.

Review

Directions: Identify the one underlined word or phrase that should be corrected or rewritten.

16 If you <u>had contacted</u> the <u>repair company</u> when the problem <u>started</u>, you
                A   B   C
<u>won't be</u> in this predicament now.
  D

17 The train <u>won't break down</u> if the regularly <u>scheduled</u> maintenance checks <u>were followed</u>.
                   A   B   C   D

18 The <u>company's</u> guarantee promised <u>that</u> the <u>fitting tubing</u> would last <u>for a minimum</u> of ten years.
           A   B   C   D

19 The <u>electrical</u> shortage <u>could have be</u> avoided <u>if the wires</u> <u>had been cleaned</u>.
           A   B   C   D

20 The optician <u>was exciting</u> by the prospect of <u>opening</u> her own store after <u>having worked</u>
                     A   B   C
for someone else for <u>over a decade</u>.
                    D

21 If they determine the <u>exact formula</u>, the company <u>would earn</u> millions from sales <u>of the product</u>.
 A   B   C   D

22 The overall <u>health</u> of the company <u>was distorting</u> by <u>the</u> group of <u>disgruntled investors</u>.
             A   B   C   D

23 If the mortgage banker <u>were</u> more available, we <u>didn't</u> have <u>so many</u> complaints <u>from his customers</u>.
                      A   B   C   D

24 The group of <u>trainees</u> <u>were fascinating</u> by the <u>demonstration</u> of the software <u>program</u>.
                 A   B   C   D

25 The project manager has <u>complaining</u> bitterly <u>if</u> the materials have <u>arrived</u> even a <u>day late</u>.
                            A   B   C   D

Reading

Part VI				
16	Ⓐ	Ⓑ	Ⓒ	Ⓓ
17	Ⓐ	Ⓑ	Ⓒ	Ⓓ
18	Ⓐ	Ⓑ	Ⓒ	Ⓓ
19	Ⓐ	Ⓑ	Ⓒ	Ⓓ
20	Ⓐ	Ⓑ	Ⓒ	Ⓓ
21	Ⓐ	Ⓑ	Ⓒ	Ⓓ
22	Ⓐ	Ⓑ	Ⓒ	Ⓓ
23	Ⓐ	Ⓑ	Ⓒ	Ⓓ
24	Ⓐ	Ⓑ	Ⓒ	Ⓓ
25	Ⓐ	Ⓑ	Ⓒ	Ⓓ

PART VII

Strategy A

Use the questions and answers to focus on an action that is being taken for a specific reason. Read the questions and answer choices before you read the passage.

Ask yourself: *"What is happening and why?"*

Why was the notice written?
(A)   Because the number of accidents is low
(B)   Because the lists are outdated
(C)   Because everyone is supposed to lower the number of accidents
(D)   Because employees have forgotten the safety procedures

Notice

Each division is being asked to look carefully at its safety record and to take action to improve it. In the last five years, there have been only two accidents in our post-production department. While that sounds very good, we can do better. The accidents that did occur were machinery-related accidents that could have been prevented. As a result, I am asking all of you to create a detailed list of the steps taken before and after use of all machinery, in order to identify areas in which we can improve our safety procedures.

All the answer choices begin with the word *because*, but note that *because* does not appear in the notice.

Which answer choices can you eliminate? (A) is illogical; a low number of accidents is a good thing. (B) *Lists* are mentioned in the passage; however there is nothing said about them being out of date. (D) This isn't mentioned in the passage and so can be eliminated. Therefore the correct answer is (C).

Task A

Identify possible reasons

Cross out those answer choices that do NOT identify a possible reason.

1   The supervisor was fired.
   - (A)   The control room was left unlocked overnight.
   - (B)   He had been working for fifteen years.
   - (C)   The computer system failed five times in two weeks and no one was notified.
   - (D)   He decided to file a lawsuit for unlawful dismissal.

2   The first biogenetically produced corn was taken out of supermarkets.
   - (A)   As a result, the company went bankrupt.
   - (B)   It was developed by scientists in a New York laboratory.
   - (C)   Severe gastrointestinal side effects were discovered.
   - (D)   The corn was prohibitively expensive.

3   They weren't able to maintain their on-line connection when the telephone rang.
   - (A)   They had an outdated system.
   - (B)   They omitted a step in the process.
   - (C)   They gave up and bought a cellular phone.
   - (D)   They called the help line to solve the problem.

4   The painter became ill and was rushed to the hospital.
   - (A)   She forgot her face mask at home and had painted without it.
   - (B)   The doctors said that within a few hours she would be fine.
   - (C)   A new type of paint was being used.
   - (D)   She hadn't eaten all day.

Strategy B

Read the questions, answer choices, and passage quickly to identify a planned action. Sometimes, but not always, the planned action will be indicated by the future tense.

What will be the result of the report?
(A)   Restaurants will become cleaner.
(B)   More restaurants will open in the city.
(C)   More employees will work for the organization.
(D)   70% of the restaurants will be closed.

According to our latest records, 30% of the restaurants in the greater metropolitan area have received a rating of 2.5 or lower on their health inspections. A passing score for our purposes is 2.75. The number of restaurants not passing inspection has increased 10% in the last 2 years.

This trend, coupled with the increasing number of new restaurants, indicates the necessity for increased vigilance to protect the health of restaurant diners. Therefore, we will be hiring and training an additional 20 inspectors for our staff. The hiring will be complete by June 30.

(C) is the correct answer. All of the answer choices include the future tense indicated by *will*. You can eliminate choices by comparing the verb tense in the answer choice with the tense in the passage. Answer choice (A) is not mentioned in the report. It may be what the organization hopes for, but it is not stated. The passage says that the number of restaurants has *already* increased. This is not a projection for the future. Therefore, answer choice (B) can be eliminated. The report indicates that 30% of the restaurants may be closed, not 70%. Therefore, eliminate answer choice (D). Answer choice (C), which is directly stated in the passage, is the planned action of the report.

Task B

Identify a planned action

Cross out those choices which can NOT be a planned action.

5   A manager is unhappy with worker efficiency.
   (A)   He will write a report.
   (B)   He received a good review.
   (C)   He will arrange a plant visit.
   (D)   He is developing an interview form.

6   An engineer can't identify the source of a leak.
   (A)   The water is cold.
   (B)   She will run a series of tests.
   (C)   She will talk to the employees.
   (D)   15 gallons have been collected.

7   The company is unhappy with its information system.
   (A)   They will investigate new potential providers.
   (B)   The systems were installed five years ago.
   (C)   The engineers tend to favor the current systems.
   (D)   Modifications will be made.

8   Production has no inventory of its best-selling CD ROM.
   (A)   It sells for $25.
   (B)   Last year, over 25,000 units were sold.
   (C)   An emergency print run is being scheduled.
   (D)   It will be taken off the shelves.

9   *Best Supplies* has to replace its toner every month.
   (A)   Too many copies are being made.
   (B)   A counter will be installed on the machines.
   (C)   Business is great.
   (D)   The competition closed for the summer.

10   The water registers an unacceptable amoebic count.
   (A)   Swimmers will be warned.
   (B)   Beaches will be closed.
   (C)   Tourism will increase this summer.
   (D)   Amoebae are not considered dangerous.

Review

Directions: Read the e-mail and choose the one best answer (A), (B), (C) or (D) to each question.

Questions 11–14 refer to the following e-mail.

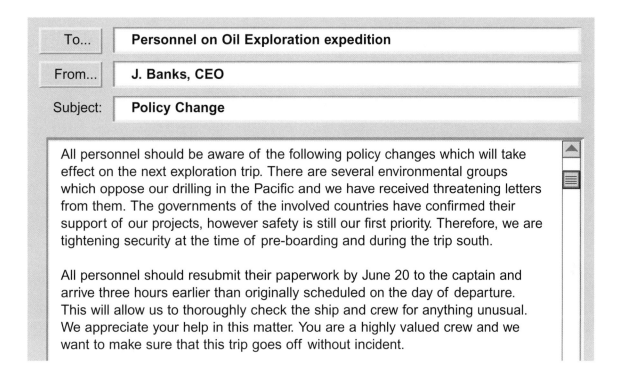

To...	**Personnel on Oil Exploration expedition**
From...	**J. Banks, CEO**
Subject:	**Policy Change**

All personnel should be aware of the following policy changes which will take effect on the next exploration trip. There are several environmental groups which oppose our drilling in the Pacific and we have received threatening letters from them. The governments of the involved countries have confirmed their support of our projects, however safety is still our first priority. Therefore, we are tightening security at the time of pre-boarding and during the trip south.

All personnel should resubmit their paperwork by June 20 to the captain and arrive three hours earlier than originally scheduled on the day of departure. This will allow us to thoroughly check the ship and crew for anything unusual. We appreciate your help in this matter. You are a highly valued crew and we want to make sure that this trip goes off without incident.

11   Why is the crew being asked to show up early?

(A) To be inspected
(B) To store the drilling equipment
(C) To meet the new crew members
(D) To turn in their documentation

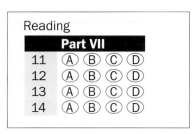

12   Who is opposed to the exploration?

(A) The new crew
(B) Environmentalists
(C) The oil company
(D) The host countries

13   What is the oil company doing in response to the threat?

(A) Canceling the trip
(B) Ignoring the threat
(C) Tightening security
(D) Resubmitting their proposals

14   Why has the company sent out the notice?

(A) To scare away the environmentalists
(B) To change the ship's personnel
(C) To alert the crew of changes
(D) To inform the governments of their plans

Listening comprehension PART I

Strategy A

Look at the pictures and quickly make a list of possible actions.
Ask yourself *what* might be happening.

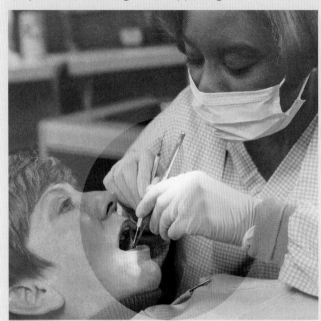

What is happening?

The dentist is examining the patient.
The dentist is filling a cavity.
The woman is having her teeth cleaned.

What is happening?

They are shaking hands.
They are greeting each other.
They are saying good-bye.

Task A

Identify the action

**Match the professions with the most appropriate action and the object of the action.
Then write a sentence using words from the three columns.**

	Professions	Action	Object
1	dentist....*B*..... ...*J*...	(A) trim	(F) patients
	A dentist drilled my tooth yesterday.		
2	pharmacist	(B) drill	(G) the latest news
3	reporter	(C) fill out	(H) a prescription
4	nurse	(D) broadcast	(I) hair
5	hair stylist	(E) take care of	(J) tooth

Strategy B

Identify possible reasons by asking yourself *why*. The answer to the question *why* will help you focus on listening for the correct answer choice and eliminate those choices which are not possible.

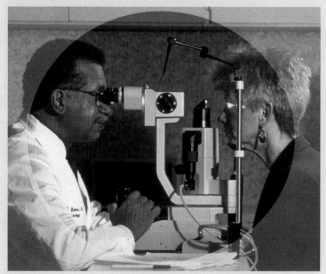

Why?
Possible reasons:
1   She is having her annual eye check up.
2   The doctor is examining her vision.
3   She is getting a new prescription for eye glasses.
4   She is experiencing problems with her eyes.

Look at the answer choices for this picture. Notice how they use words you might find in your list of reasons.
  (A) She has a definite vision of the company's future.
  (B) She needs to buy another set of water glasses.
  (C) She is having problems with her vision.
  (D) Her check-up was scheduled for last month.

The correct answer is (C).

Why?
Possible reasons:
1   The car is stuck in traffic.
2   The driver has just hit the car in front of him.
3   The man is late for a meeting.
4   The man hates driving.

Look at the answer choices for this picture. Notice how they use words you might find in your list of reasons.
  (A) The car show had a lot of pedestrian traffic.
  (B) He is on his way to a lunch meeting.
  (C) He has been the driving force behind the new product line.
  (D) His car has been at the mechanics for over a month.

The correct answer is (B).

Task B 📷

Identify a possible reason

Read the context and listen to the sentences. Mark P for the sentence that is possible and NP for the sentence that is not possible.

6   Context: A man holding a hand to his chest
   (A) ......
   (B) ......

7   Context: A runner crossing the finishing line
   (A) ......
   (B) ......

8   Context: People boating on a lake
   (A) ......
   (B) ......

9   Context: A woman making a phone call
   (A) ......
   (B) ......

10   Context: A man relaxing by a pool
   (A) ......
   (B) ......

Review

Directions: Listen to the statements and choose the one that best describes what you see in the picture.

11

12

13

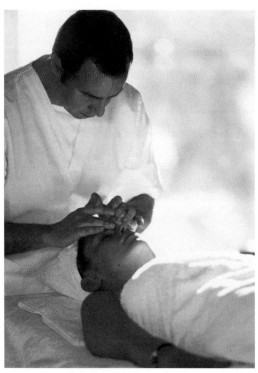

14

Listening Comprehension

Part I

11	Ⓐ	Ⓑ	Ⓒ	Ⓓ
12	Ⓐ	Ⓑ	Ⓒ	Ⓓ
13	Ⓐ	Ⓑ	Ⓒ	Ⓓ
14	Ⓐ	Ⓑ	Ⓒ	Ⓓ

PART II

Strategy A

Listen for questions that begin with *what* to ask for a result. Eliminate answer choices that do not explain a result.

What was Ms. Smith unable to do today because of her illness?
What effect did Mr. Mark's temper have on his staff?
What was the result of their arriving late?
What problems did the delay cause?

Task A

Identify a result

Cross out the answer choices that do NOT identify a result.

1   Ms. Markel returned the books to the library a week late.
What happened because the books were overdue?
(A)   She paid the librarian a small fine.
(B)   She just got back from vacation.
(C)   She borrowed the books from a friend.

2   He decided to subscribe to the business journal.
What was the result of his receiving the publication?
(A)   There was a promotional price.
(B)   It is a very expensive publication.
(C)   Everyone in the office referred to articles in the magazine.

3   She was unable to reach her supervisor.
What was the result of her efforts?
(A)   All personnel must now provide contact information when traveling.
(B)   He is over six feet tall and can easily reach the top shelf.
(C)   The supervisor is on a business trip until next week.

4   Mr. Sala has been watching what he eats.
What could happen to his health if he doesn't?
(A)   His main course looks delicious.
(B)   His family has a history of heart problems.
(C)   His doctor told him he could have a heart attack.

5   The post office has changed its hours.
What was the result of the new hours?
(A)   It is now open until 7:00 p.m.
(B)   We sent the letter hours ago.
(C)   More stamps were sold.

6   The directions to the reception were taken down from the wall.
What happened after the directions were removed?
(A)   No one ever follows directions.
(B)   Many people got lost and had to ask directions.
(C)   It's a very easy recipe to follow.

7   Azra went to see a physician about her sleeping habits.
What effect did the visit to the doctor have on her?
(A)   She can't fall asleep even when she is exhausted.
(B)   The doctor was sleepy after the large meal.
(C)   She took the pills prescribed and was able to sleep.

8   The coffee shop in our building sent us a coupon for a free lunch.
What was the result of the coupons?
(A)   There is no such thing as a free lunch.
(B)   The shop was able to double its business.
(C)   The coffee is from Guatemala.

9   The director has been very busy.
What problems did the director's schedule cause?
(A)   Important meetings were cancelled or rescheduled.
(B)   Associates could not get her approval for their plans.
(C)   She is changing her appointment calendar.

10   The clinic may have to close next month.
What effect will the closing have on its patients?
(A)   The hospital is being renovated next month.
(B)   Most patients will have to find another clinic.
(C)   The doctors will close the cabinets.

Strategy B

Listen for answer choices that include quantities and costs.
Listen for numbers as well as a unit of measure.

Heights: *5 feet, 2 inches, 1 meter, 80 centimeters*

Solid measurements: *one and a half pounds of cheese, 200 grams of ham*

Liquid measurements: *half a gallon of milk, 2 liters of beer*

Temperatures: *20 degrees Celsius, 32 degrees Fahrenheit*

Major Currencies: *Canadian Dollar, Euro, Peso, Pound (sterling), Real, US Dollar, Yuan, Yen*

Real Spoken English

Two major measuring systems are used throughout the world. Familiarity with common vocabulary items, such as *pounds, kilograms, Fahrenheit,* and *Celsius,* will help your comprehension on the TOEIC® test.

Task B

Identify costs and quantities

Complete the sentences with the words (A–E).

(A)   percent
(B)   pounds
(C)   feet
(D)   liters
(E)   Fahrenheit

11   He bought five .... of wine for the picnic.

12   The price of the sports utility vehicle rose by only three ....

13   She had gained over five .... at her last doctor's visit.

14   At six .... four inches, he was the tallest man on the office basketball team.

15   The temperature is expected to reach ninety-five degrees .... by mid-week.

Review

Directions: Listen and choose the best response to each question.

Listening Comprehension		
Part II		
16	Ⓐ Ⓑ Ⓒ	
17	Ⓐ Ⓑ Ⓒ	
18	Ⓐ Ⓑ Ⓒ	
19	Ⓐ Ⓑ Ⓒ	
20	Ⓐ Ⓑ Ⓒ	
21	Ⓐ Ⓑ Ⓒ	
22	Ⓐ Ⓑ Ⓒ	
23	Ⓐ Ⓑ Ⓒ	
24	Ⓐ Ⓑ Ⓒ	
25	Ⓐ Ⓑ Ⓒ	

PART III

Strategy A

Use the questions and answers to identify the speaker. Look for questions that begin with *who*. They will usually ask you to identify the speaker or others who are referred to in the talk. Listen carefully to the order and the sex of speakers in the conversation. As you listen to the conversation, ask yourself who the speakers are and what their relationship is.

> *Who* are the speakers?
> *Who* will attend the meeting?
> *Who* made the international phone call?

Task A 📼

Identify the speaker

Listen and identify the speakers by marking *M* for man and *W* for woman. Then choose the most likely occupation or relationship of the speakers.

1   First speaker ....M....
    Second speaker ...W.....

    The first speaker is probably a
    (A)   clothing store clerk.
    (B)   restaurant manager.
    (C)   shopper. ✓
    (D)   security guard.

2   First speaker ....
    Second speaker ....

    The first speaker is probably a
    (A)   doctor.
    (B)   receptionist.
    (C)   vendor.
    (D)   patient of Dr. Woo.

3   First speaker ....
    Second speaker ....

    The speakers are probably
    (A)   employees at a movie theater.
    (B)   co-workers.
    (C)   manager and new employee.
    (D)   producer and actor.

4   First speaker ....
    Second speaker ....

    The first speaker is probably
    (A)   considering the surgery.
    (B)   a relative of the second speaker.
    (C)   an optometrist.
    (D)   disappointed in the procedure.

5   First speaker ....
    Second speaker ....

    The second speaker is probably
    (A)   a saleswoman.
    (B)   a cafe waitress.
    (C)   a receptionist.
    (D)   Mr. Sato's boss.

Strategy B

Look for questions that ask to identify intentions. Pay attention to questions that begin with *what*. Then as you listen to the conversation, ask yourself what the intentions of the speaker or speakers are.

> *What* are they planning to do?
> *What* will the woman buy?
> *What* does the customer want to try?

Task B 📼

Identify intentions

Read the answer choices, then listen to a line from a conversation. Then cross out the answer choices that are NOT possible.

6   What is the speaker's intention?
  - (A) To go shopping for food.
  - (B) To learn ways to prepare meat dishes.
  - (C) To drive to the restaurant alone.
  - (D) To meet a friend for dinner.

7   What will the speaker do?
  - (A) Offer the fish at a lower quality.
  - (B) Buy the fish somewhere else.
  - (C) Purchase some of the food.
  - (D) Design an advertising campaign about seafood.

8   What will the speaker do?
  - (A) Learn to play tennis.
  - (B) Tell her parents thank you.
  - (C) Give her parents tennis classes.
  - (D) Give her children classes at an early age.

9   What should the woman do?
  - (A) Take some aspirin.
  - (B) Get a haircut.
  - (C) Get a headband.
  - (D) See a physician.

Review 📼

Directions: Listen and choose the best answer to each question.

10   What will the man probably do?
  - (A) Buy some new books.
  - (B) Form his own group.
  - (C) Send out information.
  - (D) Attend the next meeting.

11   What does the woman want the man to do?
  - (A) Go to the doctor.
  - (B) Tell her the time of day.
  - (C) Take her to the doctor.
  - (D) Tell her about his problems.

12   What is the man's relationship with Giovanni?
  - (A) They're co-workers.
  - (B) He's his relative.
  - (C) He's his supervisor.
  - (D) They're good friends.

13   What does the man want to do?
  - (A) Impress Charlotte.
  - (B) Give Charlotte more work.
  - (C) Send her home.
  - (D) Help her feel better.

Listening Comprehension
Part III
10 Ⓐ Ⓑ Ⓒ Ⓓ
11 Ⓐ Ⓑ Ⓒ Ⓓ
12 Ⓐ Ⓑ Ⓒ Ⓓ
13 Ⓐ Ⓑ Ⓒ Ⓓ

PART IV

Strategy A

Use the questions and answers to focus on the time. In the short talks, listen for numbers which indicate time. Pay close attention to the words surrounding the numbers which add details to the time.

> We'll meet *just before* seven o'clock.
> Dr. Lau works *substantially more than* forty hours a week.
> He usually arrives *between* mid-morning and noon.

Test Note

In the United States, time is almost always referred to using a twelve-hour clock. However, on the TOEIC test you may hear references to the 24-hour clock. Remember, 16:30 is equivalent to 4:30 p.m.

Task A

Identify time

Put the times in order (1 = earliest / shortest, 3 = latest / longest).

1. A   At 16:30. ......*2*......
   B   A little after noon. ......*1*......
   C   In the evening. ......*3*......

2. A   It ran for over thirty minutes. ....
   B   It was exactly a half an hour. ....
   C   It was a little short of thirty minutes. ....

3. A   We'll start at half past seven. ....
   B   We can't begin any later than quarter past seven. ....
   C   We should start at least by seven. ....

4. A   It lasted over a fortnight. ....
   B   It continued for almost two weeks. ....
   C   It carried on for close to a month. ....

5. A   You can come in any time after mid-morning. ....
   B   You should arrive after the noon rush. ....
   C   You should be here before the morning rush hour. ....

6. A   He finished in just under an hour. ....
   B   His time was seventy-five minutes exactly. ....
   C   He was clocked at sixty minutes and fifteen seconds. ....

Strategy B

Use the questions and answers to identify characteristics. There are many questions that ask for specific information on the TOEIC test. As you listen, ask yourself questions to understand and remember details and characteristics.

What kind of person is he?
What is characteristic of her work?
How would you describe the place?

Many of the answers to the questions above will include adjectives and descriptive phrases.

Task B

Identify characteristics

Cross out the answer choices which do NOT indicate a characteristic of the underlined phrase.

7   The exhibit showed <u>the artist's early work</u>.
   (A) The exhibit was a success.
   (B) The paintings were very dark.
   (C) She sold five paintings that evening.
   (D) The Parisian influence is obvious.

8   The <u>personal trainer</u> at our gym uses weight training exercises.
   (A) He combines many exercises in his workouts.
   (B) He is demanding and gets results.
   (C) The clients weren't happy with their prior trainers.
   (D) The club offers swimming and racquet sports.

9   Dr. Weschler sees patients at the <u>University Medical Center</u> and at the <u>Sawtelle office.</u>
   (A) He had to wait for forty five minutes after his appointment time.
   (B) Both locations have the most up-to-date equipment.
   (C) Fridays tend to be his busiest days.
   (D) He has been practicing for over ten years.

10 Katherine could recommend a <u>good printing company</u> for you to contact.
   (A) They finish their projects on time.
   (B) She is going to retire next year.
   (C) She has had some bad experiences with inexpensive but low-quality companies.
   (D) The quality of their graphics couldn't be better.

Review

Directions: Listen and choose the best answer to each question.

11 How long will the city blood supply last?
   (A) 2 weeks.
   (B) 10 months.
   (C) 52 weeks.
   (D) Two years.

12 Who should donate blood?
   (A) Everyone in the city.
   (B) Health care workers.
   (C) Employees in good health.
   (D) Anyone with an ill relative.

13 When will the organizational meeting take place?
   (A) On Thursday.
   (B) On Friday.
   (C) In two weeks.
   (D) In about a month.

14 What kind of players are they looking for?
   (A) Enthusiastic players.
   (B) Only experienced ball players.
   (C) Employees who played last year.
   (D) People who can teach.

Listening Comprehension			
Part IV			
11	Ⓐ Ⓑ Ⓒ Ⓓ		
12	Ⓐ Ⓑ Ⓒ Ⓓ		
13	Ⓐ Ⓑ Ⓒ Ⓓ		
14	Ⓐ Ⓑ Ⓒ Ⓓ		

Reading PART V

Strategy A

Look at the quantity words that precede the nouns and decide which words are appropriate in the situation. Many of the words have similar meanings but cannot be used in all situations.

Correct
She has *more* energy *than* the last manager.
She has *a lot of* energy.

Incorrect
She has *most* energy *than* the last manager.
(Don't use the superlative indicator *most* when comparing two items.)
She has *many* energy.
(*Many* is used for count nouns. *Energy* is a non-count noun.)

> Grammar Glossary **Quantity Words** (p219)

Task A

Identify the correct quantity word

Cross out the words that are NOT possible.

1   She always eats .... fruit for breakfast.
    (A) much
    (B) many pieces of
    (C) a lot of
    (D) most

2   His co-workers didn't know that he had ....
    serious problems.
    (A) several
    (B) a few
    (C) couple
    (D) some

3   New technology has changed the way that
    .... of us communicate.
    (A) much
    (B) the majority
    (C) most
    (D) more

4   .... of the dentist's patients are unhappy
    with the new billing policy.
    (A) A couple
    (B) Some
    (C) Few
    (D) Any

5   Mr. Barber has .... clients than anyone else
    in the firm.
    (A) more
    (B) most
    (C) a lot of
    (D) many

6   The prices fell .... what was expected.
    (A) fewer than
    (B) less than
    (C) a little
    (D) least

Strategy B

Read the sentences and answer choices quickly looking for adverbs. The adverbs will give information about verb phrases. The word may be an adverb if it answers:

How? How often? When? Where? Why?

Grammar Glossary **Adverbs** (p212)

Task B

Identify the adverbs

Choose the correct form of the word and complete the sentence. Then write another sentence with the other form of the word.

good / well

7   He felt .... enough to return to work a week after leaving the hospital.

....

hard / hardly

8   Ms. Kang .... recognized the manager that she worked for five years ago.

....

extreme / extremely

9   She is .... talented as a gymnast.

....

annual / annually

10 We visit the doctor .... for a physical examination.

....

bad / badly

11 Even with his torn ligament, Dale didn't finish the race as .... as his coach had feared.

....

Review

Directions: Choose the one word or phrase that best completes the sentence.

12 She continued to receive .... phone calls after she left her position.
   (A) couple
   (B) handful of
   (C) some
   (D) a several

13 The company always receives .... packages after the holidays.
   (A) a most
   (B) lot
   (C) much
   (D) many

14 ...., his assistant has been arriving late to work.
   (A) Late
   (B) Recently
   (C) Of lately
   (D) Recent

15 She lost .... blood that they needed to give her a transfusion.
   (A) many
   (B) a lot of
   (C) most
   (D) so much

16 If we leave .... after work, we should be able to play golf for at least three hours.
   (A) immediately
   (B) exact
   (C) immediate
   (D) short

Reading

	Part V			
12	Ⓐ	Ⓑ	Ⓒ	Ⓓ
13	Ⓐ	Ⓑ	Ⓒ	Ⓓ
14	Ⓐ	Ⓑ	Ⓒ	Ⓓ
15	Ⓐ	Ⓑ	Ⓒ	Ⓓ
16	Ⓐ	Ⓑ	Ⓒ	Ⓓ

PART VI

Strategy A

Read the sentence quickly to yourself to see if the verb + preposition combination "sounds right". This section of the TOEIC test is the place to trust your ear. If something "sounds wrong", look carefully at the preposition and try replacing it with others. The verb and preposition not only need to sound right together, but also to have the right meaning for the context.

Look at the difference:

She has *looked after* her sister since they were small children.
She has been *looking for* her sister since she was 10 years old.
She is *looking up* her sister in the phone book.

Each of the three sentences is correct. They all use the same verb but with a different preposition in each sentence. This changes the meaning of the verb each time.

Grammar Glossary **Verbs + Prepositions** (p221)

Task A

Identify the verb + preposition combinations

Match each verb with all of its possible prepositions. Then write the correct verb + preposition in the sentences.

out of up on down

count *out, count up, count on, count down* ....

check ....

cut ....

work ....

take care ....

1   The doctor told him to .... the amount of fat in his diet.

2   Ken and Koji have started to .... every day after work.

3   Alison started to .... her elderly mother last year after she fell and broke her hip.

4   He told us not to .... him for the basketball game because he had to work late.

5   The school nurse called to .... on Ali.

Strategy B

Read the sentences quickly and mark the nouns with *C* for count or *NC* for non-count and *S* for specific or *NS* for non-specific. Then check to see that an appropriate article or adjective, and verb, are used with the noun.

Noun	Count or non-count	Type of Article
the used furniture	non-count	specific
a piece of fruit	count	non-specific
the fruit	non-count	specific
the medical community	non-count	specific
some dentist's patients	count	non-specific

Grammar Glossary Nouns: Count/Non-count (p216)

Task B

Identify the count and non-count nouns and their articles

Mark the highlighted words and phrases with *C* for count or *NC* for non-count. Then underline the correct quantifier.

6   They decided to refurnish <u>the</u>/any **house** with a/<u>some</u> **furniture** that they inherited from her great aunt.
     <small>C</small> (over house)   <small>NC</small> (over furniture)

7   Her doctor failed to give her *any/some* good **reason** to continue taking *the/a* **medicine**.

8   Timothy didn't ask for *an/any* **advice**, before *the/any* **interview**.

9   Over *much/many* **years**, the nurse kept track of *a/the* health and **eating habits** of her patients.

10 *Many/The* **discovery** of large amounts of money in *the/some* **safe**, made everyone suspicious of *any/the* **store manager**.

11 Renzo submitted a request for reimbursement of *some/any* **education classes** that he took in *a/the* **fall**.

12 *A/The* **luggage** was lost somewhere between Tokyo and Sydney, so *a/the* **airlines** gave the passenger money to purchase necessities.

13 *A/The* **level of customer satisfaction** has steadily increased over *a/the* **last decade**.

14 The company initiated *a/some* **loan program** to assist its workers.

15 *The/A* **city manager** is concerned about *an/the* increasing levels of **noise** in *a/the* **city center**.

Review

Directions: Identify the one underlined word or phrase that should be corrected or rewritten.

16 Professional soccer <u>team</u> travel with an <u>extensive group</u> of <u>coaches</u>, trainers and <u>medical staff</u>.
                      A   B   C   D

17 The group <u>feels</u> that she needs to <u>concentrate from</u> her <u>communication skills</u>
                A   B   C
    if she is <u>to succeed in</u> the company.
               D

18 <u>Unfortunately</u>, the <u>only person</u> <u>who</u> can solve this <u>problems</u> is not in the office today.
        A   B   C   D

19 The <u>insurance</u> company and Mr. Chang finally <u>agreed for</u> a <u>fair price</u> for the optometrist's <u>services</u>.
         A   B   C   D

20 He <u>took a cruise</u> with <u>more than</u> $2000 he <u>had accumulated</u> <u>in coin</u>.
             A   B   C   D

21 <u>Farmers</u> from <u>around</u> the country were asked to <u>participate from</u> a forum <u>on ways to</u> increase living wages.
     A   B   C   D

22 <u>After a year</u> of intense rehabilitation, she was able <u>for</u> walk without the <u>aid of</u> a <u>cane</u> or braces.
         A   B   C   D

23 The director was <u>known for</u> <u>fighting off</u> the rights and <u>benefits</u> of his <u>employees</u>.
                     A   B   C   D

24 Everyone thought <u>it</u> odd that there was no mention <u>about</u> the hard work and
                     A   B
    <u>dedication of</u> the research group at the <u>annual</u> awards dinner.
        C   D

25 To <u>their</u> surprise, the fifteen <u>pound</u> of <u>chicken</u> was not <u>enough for</u>
       A   B   C   D
    the group of journalists and reporters.

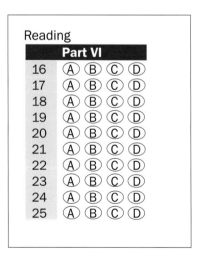

Reading

Part VI

	A	B	C	D
16	Ⓐ	Ⓑ	Ⓒ	Ⓓ
17	Ⓐ	Ⓑ	Ⓒ	Ⓓ
18	Ⓐ	Ⓑ	Ⓒ	Ⓓ
19	Ⓐ	Ⓑ	Ⓒ	Ⓓ
20	Ⓐ	Ⓑ	Ⓒ	Ⓓ
21	Ⓐ	Ⓑ	Ⓒ	Ⓓ
22	Ⓐ	Ⓑ	Ⓒ	Ⓓ
23	Ⓐ	Ⓑ	Ⓒ	Ⓓ
24	Ⓐ	Ⓑ	Ⓒ	Ⓓ
25	Ⓐ	Ⓑ	Ⓒ	Ⓓ

PART VII

We are pleased to announce that we will be the host institution for a series of lectures by the renowned career specialist, Nancy Kampf. Dr. Kampf received her doctoral degree from our university ten years ago. During that time, she has remained in close contact with the University. We are honored that we will be the first location on her lecture tour, *Making the Most of Your Career*, which is also the name of her recently published book. Dr. Kampf is perhaps best known for her wide range of interests and talents, making her a captivating speaker for the most diverse audiences. She has lived and traveled extensively in Southeast Asia, Europe and the southern cone of South America. She is fluent in five different languages, growing up in a trilingual German, Korean and English household. She has worked for three major *Fortune 500* companies and has successfully started her own publishing company along with her lecture series. As if this weren't enough, she is the devoted mother of two children. Whether you are just beginning your career or are contemplating a career change, do not miss this opportunity to hear this very talented speaker.

(B) is the correct answer.
The question asks you to find the one area in which Dr. Kampf is NOT a specialist. As you scan the announcement, eliminate answer choices. The first sentence refers to Dr. Kampf's work as a career specialist, and the name of her book refers to careers. Finding a job is closely related to careers, so you can eliminate (C). You quickly see that she speaks 5 languages, so (A) can be eliminated. A little further on, you read that she started her own business, so (D) could possibly be the correct answer. (B) Medicine may confuse you if you are not sure what a doctoral degree is, but a doctoral degree is not necessarily associated with medicine.

Task A

Identify abilities

Cross out the answer choice that does NOT describe an ability of the person.

1   The physical therapist is booked for the rest of the week.

    (A) She is over thirty years old.
    (B) She is good with people.
    (C) She understands human anatomy.
    (D) She graduated in 1990 from the state university.

2   In my opinion, the best weather reporter is on Channel 5.

    (A) She wrote the article last week.
    (B) She interprets the information in an interesting way.
    (C) It will be hot and humid.
    (D) She speaks slowly and clearly.

3   As a triathlete, he spends over twenty hours a week in training.

    (A) He participated in his first event ten years ago.
    (B) He is strong and fast.
    (C) His level of concentration is legendary.
    (D) He won the Steelman Triathalon in 1998.

4   The disc jockey is well known for his eclectic taste in music.

    (A) He writes reviews for the food column.
    (B) He is a talented interviewer.
    (C) He is very intuitive about the public's taste.
    (D) He has ridden most of the famous horses.

Strategy B

Read the passage quickly to look for items that are included in a list. The contents are sometimes identified by a listing that includes commas, other times by a series of sentences in the same paragraph. Look for questions that begin with *what*.

What is included in the report?
(A)   Stock for the employees
(B)   A plan for the next fifteen years
(C)   A look back at the best achievers
(D)   The recent changes in staffing

Memo on Xixo's Annual Report

Xixo's annual report will be released and distributed on February 1. It will be distributed to all employees and stockholders. As you know, we have had a tumultuous year, and the report will explain the reasons of the volatility. Among other things, you should look for overall performance by division, a ten-year recap of top performers, and an overview of our five-year business plan. We haven't included some of the personnel changes that are occurring now. We would ask that employees use discretion when discussing the restructuring. We are at a turning point in the industry and we must show a strong and unified front.

(C) is the correct answer.
The question asks to identify the contents of the report. Reading the memo quickly, you see in the third sentence a number of commas. That is a good place to look for content. You can eliminate (B) as it states fifteen years and not five years. Stockholders are mentioned in the second sentence, but it says nothing of distribution of stock. Therefore you can eliminate (A). The memo states that staffing or personnel changes are not mentioned, so (D) can be eliminated. This leaves (C). *Achievers* is a synonym for *performers*, and *look back* and *recap* are synonyms.

Task B

Identify contents

Cross out the words that do NOT fit.

5   physical activity
     running, swimming, reading, skiing,
     watching TV, dancing

6   annual physical
     height, blood type, blood pressure, hair cut,
     eye color, weight, cholesterol level

7   traffic report
     accidents, congested areas, drug
     manufacturers, rush hour, freeways, traffic
     jam, robberies

8   political speech
     agenda, tax cuts, lunch reservations,
     voters, police headquarters, arrests,
     promises

9   medical report
     results of study, residents, new findings,
     further examinations, aspirin, expert
     opinion, publishing house

10 business journal
     fashion, reporter, new technology,
     successful entrepreneur, suit, editorial
     section, featured company

Review

Directions: Read the e-mail and choose the one best answer (A), (B), (C) or (D) to each question.

Questions 11–14 refer to the following e-mail.

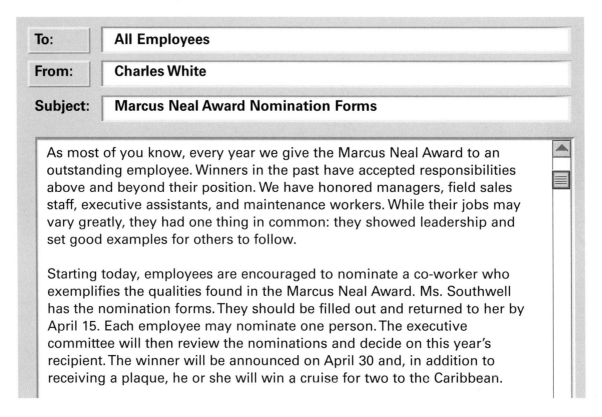

To:	**All Employees**
From:	**Charles White**
Subject:	**Marcus Neal Award Nomination Forms**

As most of you know, every year we give the Marcus Neal Award to an outstanding employee. Winners in the past have accepted responsibilities above and beyond their position. We have honored managers, field sales staff, executive assistants, and maintenance workers. While their jobs may vary greatly, they had one thing in common: they showed leadership and set good examples for others to follow.

Starting today, employees are encouraged to nominate a co-worker who exemplifies the qualities found in the Marcus Neal Award. Ms. Southwell has the nomination forms. They should be filled out and returned to her by April 15. Each employee may nominate one person. The executive committee will then review the nominations and decide on this year's recipient. The winner will be announced on April 30 and, in addition to receiving a plaque, he or she will win a cruise for two to the Caribbean.

11 What abilities will the winner demonstrate?
(A) Good nautical skills
(B) Motivating co-workers
(C) Excellent writing ability
(D) Quick decision-making

12 How much time do the employees have to make their nominations?
(A) Until April 15
(B) Until April 30
(C) Around two weeks
(D) The time period has ended

13 What will the prize include?
(A) A salary increase
(B) More responsibility
(C) A trip on a boat
(D) A job promotion

14 Who is eligible to win the award?
(A) All workers and their families
(B) Only senior managers
(C) Only maintenance workers
(D) All employees

Reading

	Part VII
11	Ⓐ Ⓑ Ⓒ Ⓓ
12	Ⓐ Ⓑ Ⓒ Ⓓ
13	Ⓐ Ⓑ Ⓒ Ⓓ
14	Ⓐ Ⓑ Ⓒ Ⓓ

Practice Test Two

Listening Comprehension

In this section of the test, you will have the chance to show how well you understand spoken English. There are four parts to this section, with special directions for each part.

PART I

Directions: For each question, you will see a picture in your test book and you will hear four short statements. The statements will be spoken just one time. They will not be printed in your test book, so you must listen carefully to understand what the speaker says.

When you hear the four statements, look at the picture in your test book and choose the statement that best describes what you see in the picture. Then, on your answer sheet, find the number of the question and mark your answer. Look at the sample below.

Sample Answer
Ⓐ ● Ⓒ Ⓓ

Now listen to the four statements.

Statement (B), "They're having a meeting," best describes what you see in the picture.
Therefore, you should choose answer (B).

GO ON TO THE NEXT PAGE

1.

2.

3.

4.

GO ON TO THE NEXT PAGE

5.

6.

7.

8.

GO ON TO THE NEXT PAGE

9.

10.

11.

12.

GO ON TO THE NEXT PAGE

13.

14.

15.

16.

GO ON TO THE NEXT PAGE

17.

18.

19.

20.

GO ON TO THE NEXT PAGE

PART II

Directions: In this part of the test, you will hear a question spoken in English, followed by three responses, also spoken in English. The question and the responses will be spoken just one time. They will not be printed in your test book, so you must listen carefully to understand what the speakers say. You are to choose the best response to each question.

Now listen to a sample question.

You will hear:

You will also hear:

Sample Answer

The best response to the question "How are you?" is choice (A), "I am fine, thank you." Therefore, you should choose answer (A).

21. Mark your answer on your answer sheet.

22. Mark your answer on your answer sheet.

23. Mark your answer on your answer sheet.

24. Mark your answer on your answer sheet.

25. Mark your answer on your answer sheet.

26. Mark your answer on your answer sheet.

27. Mark your answer on your answer sheet.

28. Mark your answer on your answer sheet.

29. Mark your answer on your answer sheet.

30. Mark your answer on your answer sheet.

31. Mark your answer on your answer sheet.

32. Mark your answer on your answer sheet.

33. Mark your answer on your answer sheet.

34. Mark your answer on your answer sheet.

35. Mark your answer on your answer sheet.

36. Mark your answer on your answer sheet.

37. Mark your answer on your answer sheet.

38. Mark your answer on your answer sheet.

39. Mark your answer on your answer sheet.

40. Mark your answer on your answer sheet.

41. Mark your answer on your answer sheet.

42. Mark your answer on your answer sheet.

43. Mark your answer on your answer sheet.

44. Mark your answer on your answer sheet.

45. Mark your answer on your answer sheet.

46. Mark your answer on your answer sheet.

47. Mark your answer on your answer sheet.

48. Mark your answer on your answer sheet.

49. Mark your answer on your answer sheet.

50. Mark your answer on your answer sheet.

PART III

Directions: In this part of the test, you will hear thirty short conversations between two people. The conversations will not be printed in your test book. You will hear the conversations only once, so you must listen carefully to understand what the speakers say.

In your test book, you will read a question about each conversation. The question will be followed by four answers. You are to choose the best answer to each question and mark it on your answer sheet.

51. When is the man going to work?

    (A) Until late tonight.
    (B) Saturday and Sunday.
    (C) Only today.
    (D) Several hours on the weekend.

52. What will happen tomorrow?

    (A) His furniture will arrive.
    (B) He will close his house.
    (C) He will unpack his belongings.
    (D) His boxes will be moved.

53. Why are the women concerned?

    (A) The suppliers can't locate the office.
    (B) The office manager isn't doing a good job.
    (C) There is no office manager.
    (D) The position isn't necessary.

54. Who saw a good game?

    (A) The man.
    (B) Evie.
    (C) The woman.
    (D) The woman's friend.

55. What do the speakers think about the new office?

    (A) They need more space.
    (B) They want privacy.
    (C) They want to have a private conversation.
    (D) They think it is a good plan.

56. What makes the woman nervous?

    (A) Certain beverages.
    (B) Her assistant, James.
    (C) Candy.
    (D) Loud noises.

57. What does the man want to do?

    (A) Go to dinner with someone else.
    (B) Postpone the event.
    (C) Cook dinner for Luciana and David.
    (D) Invite their friends for a meal.

58. Why did the man try to call the woman?

    (A) To notify her of the problem.
    (B) To fix the telephone.
    (C) To share some good information.
    (D) To introduce himself.

59. Who is Mr. Stevens?

    (A) The man's assistant.
    (B) A friend.
    (C) A colleague.
    (D) Jack's supervisor.

60. What will the men do?

    (A) Go to lunch now.
    (B) Wait for several hours.
    (C) Skip lunch to finish the project.
    (D) Leave in less than an hour.

61. What does the man suggest the woman do?

    (A) Call back.
    (B) Hang up.
    (C) Leave a voice message.
    (D) Dial another extension.

62. What does the woman want to do?

    (A) Take a holiday.
    (B) Vacate the offices.
    (C) Move in a few months.
    (D) Make a vacation schedule.

GO ON TO THE NEXT PAGE

63. Where did the man see Ann?

    (A) In the hall.
    (B) At a conference.
    (C) On vacation.
    (D) In a hotel.

64. What does the man want to do?

    (A) Earn more money.
    (B) Postpone the product release.
    (C) Build the company's image.
    (D) Start selling the product as scheduled.

65. What is typical weather for the time of year?

    (A) Hot, dry weather.
    (B) Sunny days.
    (C) Snow.
    (D) Rainy and cold.

66. Which form of transportation are people likely to take during a strike?

    (A) Subway.
    (B) Cars.
    (C) Buses.
    (D) Trains.

67. Who will receive the report in the morning?

    (A) Carl.
    (B) Sherry.
    (C) Roger.
    (D) Both speakers.

68. How will the council vote on the port?

    (A) Only the construction companies know.
    (B) It will most likely be rejected.
    (C) It is uncertain as some groups are against it.
    (D) The project will definitely be approved.

69. What is the problem?

    (A) There is no record of the man's reservation.
    (B) The man's party hasn't arrived.
    (C) The man couldn't speak with the owner.
    (D) Dana McCain is late.

70. Where is this conversation most likely taking place?

    (A) At the airport.
    (B) At a hotel restaurant.
    (C) At the front desk.
    (D) In the guest's room.

71. When will the move occur?

    (A) Later than expected.
    (B) At the end of the month.
    (C) Before the computers are set up.
    (D) During the construction.

72. How do the women feel about Marketing News?

    (A) It doesn't have very interesting articles.
    (B) It's nothing informative.
    (C) They like the topics.
    (D) Everyone must read it.

73. What happened to Mike?

    (A) He was in an accident.
    (B) He was late for work.
    (C) He sold his car last night.
    (D) He couldn't find the hospital.

74. What are the men discussing?

    (A) A lost ID card.
    (B) Poor security measures.
    (C) A part-time employee.
    (D) The design of the building.

75. What is true about the restaurant?

    (A) It is busy.
    (B) It has a reserved atmosphere.
    (C) It is spacious.
    (D) It's in France.

76. What does the woman say?

    (A) She will accompany the man.
    (B) Mario's directions are always good.
    (C) She will meet the man in two days.
    (D) The center is difficult to find.

77. Where does this conversation take place?

    (A) At an art gallery.
    (B) At a cinema.
    (C) At a photo-processing shop.
    (D) At a movie studio.

78. Where does the man's trip originate?

    (A) Turkey.
    (B) Los Angeles.
    (C) Paris.
    (D) Ankara.

79. What will the man do now?

    (A) Finish his work.
    (B) Leave the office.
    (C) Meet with the woman.
    (D) Schedule a 10 a.m. meeting.

80. What are the speakers preparing for?

    (A) A rainy day.
    (B) A busy meeting.
    (C) Taking a shower.
    (D) The end of a storm.

GO ON TO THE NEXT PAGE

Directions: In this part of the test, you will hear several short talks. Each will be spoken just one time. They will not be printed in your test book, so you must listen carefully to understand and remember what is said.

In your test book, you will read two or more questions about each short talk. The questions will be followed by four answers. You are to choose the best answer to each question and mark it on your answer sheet.

81. When is the speaker talking?

    (A) Just before 9:00.
    (B) In the morning.
    (C) After 7:00.
    (D) In the afternoon.

82. What is the purpose of the event?

    (A) To open a new store.
    (B) To introduce a new music group.
    (C) To hire new employees.
    (D) To raise money.

83. To whom is the talk directed?

    (A) The new office manager.
    (B) Current employees.
    (C) The workers at Dextech.
    (D) A group of accountants.

84. When will the move take place?

    (A) They'll begin today.
    (B) This week.
    (C) In approximately four weeks.
    (D) In a few months.

85. To whom is Bob speaking?

    (A) Faculty members.
    (B) Sports professionals.
    (C) Potential members.
    (D) His employees.

86. What does the organization offer?

    (A) Complimentary clothes.
    (B) Free tennis equipment.
    (C) Tennis classes.
    (D) Swimming lessons.

87. What type of company is Instant Marketing?

    (A) Small.
    (B) New.
    (C) Failing.
    (D) Expanding.

88. What is the purpose of the talk?

    (A) To introduce a company's product.
    (B) To recruit representatives.
    (C) To open an office in a new country.
    (D) To improve customer service.

89. What can participants do at the end of the talk?

    (A) Complete an application.
    (B) Answer the speaker's questions.
    (C) Have an interview.
    (D) Take a tour of the company.

90. Who is most likely listening to the talk?

    (A) Vegetarians.
    (B) Bankers.
    (C) Statisticians.
    (D) Meat producers.

91. Why is Mr. Neal well known?

    (A) He sells excellent beef.
    (B) He successfully advertises.
    (C) He campaigns against meat consumption.
    (D) He was elected in 2002.

92. Where does this announcement take place?

    (A) On a plane.
    (B) In a government building.
    (C) At an immigration office.
    (D) On a train.

93. What are the listeners asked to do?

    (A) Show identification.
    (B) Move to another area.
    (C) Buy local fruits.
    (D) Exit in thirty minutes.

94. What is the series of talks about?

    (A) Career advancement.
    (B) Designing office space.
    (C) Outdoor living.
    (D) Office furniture.

95. According to the speaker, what has happened in the workplace?

    (A) Not much has changed.
    (B) Individual offices were more common in the past.
    (C) Cubicles are a thing of the past.
    (D) Space has become less effective.

96. How many designers will speak?

    (A) Six.
    (B) Two.
    (C) Three.
    (D) Five.

97. What will happen at the end of the talk?

    (A) Everyone will watch videos.
    (B) The speakers will discuss the last 50 years.
    (C) The experts will create a new space.
    (D) Participants will go on a walking tour.

98. How many projects were entered in the contest?

    (A) Almost 5000.
    (B) More than 500.
    (C) Only 5.
    (D) Less than 50.

99. What is the purpose of this announcement?

    (A) To announce the beginning of a contest.
    (B) To honor last year's winners.
    (C) To announce the winners.
    (D) To promote a city in Switzerland.

100. Why will the winners go to Bern?

    (A) In order to visit the main office.
    (B) To present their proposals to the judges.
    (C) So that they can develop their ideas.
    (D) In order to manufacture their products.

This is the end of the Listening Comprehension portion of Practice Test Two.
Turn to Part V in your test book.

GO ON TO THE NEXT PAGE

YOU WILL HAVE ONE HOUR AND FIFTEEN MINUTES TO COMPLETE PARTS V, VI AND VII OF THE TEST.

Reading

In this section of the test, you will have a chance to show how well you understand written English. There are three parts to this section, with special directions for each part.

PART V

Directions: **Questions 101–140** are incomplete sentences. Four words or phrases, marked (A), (B), (C), (D) are given beneath each sentence. You are to choose the one word or phrase that best complete the sentence. Then, on your answer sheet, find the number of the question and mark your answer.

You will read:
    Because the equipment is very delicate,
    it must be handled with ....

    (A) caring
    (B) careful
    (C) care
    (D) carefully

Sample Answer
Ⓐ Ⓑ ● Ⓓ

The sentence should read, "Because the equipment is very delicate, it must be handled with care." Therefore, you should choose answer (C).

Now begin work on the questions.

---

101. A special event is being planned to show .... for the employees.

    (A) appreciate
    (B) appreciation
    (C) appreciated
    (D) appreciating

102. Bancasia's .... lies in its loyal and dedicated employees.

    (A) strong
    (B) strength
    (C) stronger
    (D) strengthening

103. Industry leaders believe that the beverage company needs to reinvent ....

    (A) itself
    (B) themselves
    (C) herself
    (D) ourselves

104. The financial .... suggested an international mutual fund.

    (A) advise
    (B) advising
    (C) advice
    (D) advisor

105. Employees from around the world can .... the material at the same time.

    (A) access
    (B) agree
    (C) adhere
    (D) administer

106. .... a top manager is a matter of skill, not of luck.

    (A) Been
    (B) Be
    (C) Being
    (D) Are

107. The .... will be pushed back for a third time.

(A) extension
(B) final
(C) deadline
(D) goal

108. .... of the Olympic Games feel that they are too professional.

(A) Critic
(B) Critical
(C) Criticism
(D) Critics

109. The bridge .... the east and west parts of the city will be repaired next year.

(A) contacting
(B) corresponding
(C) connecting
(D) combining

110. The continuing .... in the region is negatively affecting the economy.

(A) violation
(B) violence
(C) velocity
(D) variation

111. The team turned .... in at noon on Friday and then took the afternoon off.

(A) someone
(B) anything
(C) everything
(D) nowhere

112. The executive somehow finds time to volunteer at the .... school.

(A) near
(B) local
(C) close
(D) neighbor

113. .... buying the furniture, the new owners decided to lease it.

(A) Unless
(B) In spite of
(C) Besides
(D) Instead of

114. The closure of the Tokyo office came .... a surprise to everyone.

(A) as
(B) of
(C) on
(D) by

115. Even though the new employee graduated from a top university, she had very little .... experience.

(A) practice
(B) practicing
(C) practical
(D) practices

116. Employees are .... to go to the company physician for an annual check-up.

(A) established
(B) encouraged
(C) enacted
(D) effected

117. Mr. Arcilla was removed from his .... when it was discovered that classified documents were missing.

(A) hold
(B) position
(C) arrangement
(D) rank

118. Safety eyewear must be .... at all times upon entering this area of the factory.

(A) wear
(B) worn
(C) wore
(D) wearing

GO ON TO THE NEXT PAGE

119. The director made sure that she hadn't forgotten anything .... vacating the office.

(A) during
(B) in between
(C) before
(D) after

120. .... they anticipated finishing the job in four weeks, it dragged on for over four months.

(A) If
(B) Because
(C) Since
(D) Although

121. She needs to buy a more powerful computer for home so that she can be in .... communication with her European colleagues.

(A) constant
(B) always
(C) persistent
(D) even

122. Rodney is .... to return from Egypt on Friday afternoon.

(A) expected
(B) expects
(C) expectant
(D) expectation

123. After the merger, they discovered that they needed to hire .... workers.

(A) most
(B) any
(C) more
(D) least

124. The report indicates that even .... attention needs to be paid to hiring practices.

(A) closer
(B) closed
(C) closing
(D) close

125. .... the last year, a number of upscale restaurants and shops have opened in the area.

(A) Around
(B) Approximately
(C) Whereby
(D) Almost

126. Twenty years ago there was a .... of health care professionals while today there is a shortage.

(A) surplus
(B) deficiency
(C) redundant
(D) scarcity

127. Being new .... the area, he didn't know the morning rush hour traffic patterns.

(A) as
(B) of
(C) at
(D) to

128. Through a referral, she found a dentist who was .... patient and gentle.

(A) both
(B) twice
(C) and
(D) pair

129. Warren .... that he did not share responsibility during the beginning of the project.

(A) admonished
(B) addressed
(C) adhered
(D) admitted

130. The .... from the airport to the city center are listed on the window by the information desk.

(A) bills
(B) checks
(C) rates
(D) invoices

131. .... our performance this last quarter, no one should expect more than a 3% salary increase.

(A) In spite of
(B) Without
(C) By
(D) Because

132. Passengers often complain that there is, in fact, too .... food during the cruise.

(A) many
(B) few
(C) much
(D) less

133. Twice a year the showroom is open to the .... public.

(A) extensive
(B) general
(C) broad
(D) common

134. The software problem resulted in more than 500 delayed .... canceled flights in the region.

(A) if
(B) since
(C) but
(D) or

135. The opera company will make its final .... tonight before starting a month-long Asian tour.

(A) appear
(B) appearance
(C) appeared
(D) appearing

136. DRA has now surpassed .... competitors in spending on research and development.

(A) its
(B) his
(C) their
(D) our

137. The French .... company is trying to enter the Asian market.

(A) medium
(B) media
(C) meditate
(D) medicate

138. She was .... to reach Janet, but was unable to because she had the wrong phone number.

(A) tried
(B) try
(C) tries
(D) trying

139. The new employee is the first to arrive in the morning and the .... to leave in the evening.

(A) end
(B) last
(C) previous
(D) finish

140. The team of managers quickly brought the crisis .... control.

(A) in
(B) under
(C) about
(D) with

GO ON TO THE NEXT PAGE

PART VI

Directions: In **Questions 141–160**, each sentence has four words or phrases underlined. The four underlined parts of the sentence are marked (A), (B), (C), (D). You are to identify the **one** underlined word or phrase that should be corrected or rewritten. Then, on your answer sheet, find the number of the question and mark your answer.

Example:

Sample Answer
● Ⓑ Ⓒ Ⓓ

All <u>employee</u> are required <u>to wear</u> their
     A   B
<u>identification</u> badges <u>while</u> at work.
     C   D

The underlined word "employee" is not correct in this sentence. This sentence should read, "All employees are required to wear their identification badges while at work." Therefore, you should choose answer (A).
Now begin work on the questions.

---

141. The group <u>of engineers</u> currently <u>are trying</u> to
            A   B
reduce <u>the amount of noise</u> <u>from</u> the airport.
           C   D

142. <u>Their</u> continuing <u>financial support</u> <u>is critical</u> to our
     A   B   C
<u>succeed</u>.
 D

143. <u>Organic foods</u> are <u>more expensive</u> to produce
      A   B
<u>that</u> conventional <u>ones</u>.
 C   D

144. <u>More than 75%</u> <u>of the employees</u> surveyed <u>are</u>
      A   B   C
highly <u>satisfied for</u> their jobs.
       D

145. <u>Economists</u> are concerned <u>that</u>, as oil prices <u>rise</u>,
     A   B   C
oil reserves <u>would grow</u> too large.
         D

146. Workers <u>from</u> fifty years <u>ago</u> would not <u>be able to</u>
           A   B   C
recognize <u>today</u> workplace.
        D

147. <u>All</u> advertisements <u>must be</u> approved <u>at</u> Grace
    A   B   C
Chun, the <u>marketing director</u>.
          D

148. The founders of the company, <u>they</u> are
                          A
<u>flying in from</u> Europe and will work <u>at</u> the North
       B   C
American office <u>for a week</u>.
           D

149. Even if she is a close friend of the director,
      A   B
she still lost her job when the company
         C
reduced the number of employees.
   D

150. The coalition of business owners is request a cut
          A   B   C
in property taxes.
   D

151. Because of her many years of service, Patricia,
      A
she was permitted to take a six month
B
leave of absence starting at year's end.
         C   D

152. Mr. Rose always has the packages sent to the
                                      A
main Seoul office why they are then distributed
                  B   C   D
to the branch offices.

153. Several air traffic controllers are under investigated
      A   B   C
for the jet accident.
           D

154. While the factory hasn't updated its equipment,
      A   B
it can't produce the necessary amounts.
C   D

155. The frequent business traveler can quick
        A   B
accumulate miles and points for future travel.
    C   D

156. As you know, the Parren Group is dedicated to
      A   B
rewarding an excellent young business leaders.
         C   D

157. Everyone in the office put on long hours for two
      A   B
weeks in order to finish the project on time.
        C   D

158. Certain banks place limits on the amount of
      A   B
money that a customer can withdrawn from a
        C   D
retirement account.

159. The accountants work many hours in March than
      A   B
they do in any other month.
  C   D

160. Without an drastic change in the markets,
          A   B
the mutual fund will do poorly this year.
   C   D

GO ON TO THE NEXT PAGE

PART VII

Directions: Questions 161–200 are based on a selection of reading materials, such as notices, letters, forms, newspaper and magazine articles, and advertisements. You are to choose the **one** best answer (A), (B), (C) or (D) to each question. Then, on your answer sheet, find the number of the question and mark your answer. Answer all questions following each reading selection on the basis of what is **stated** or **implied** in that section.

Read the following example.

> The Museum of Technology is a "hands-on" museum, designed for people to experience science at work. Visitors are encouraged to use, test, and handle the objects on display. Special demonstrations are scheduled for the first and second Wednesdays of each month at 13:30. Open Tuesday–Friday 12:00–16:30, Saturday 10:00–17:30, and Sunday 11:00–16:30.
>
> When during the month can visitors see special demonstrations?
>
> *Sample Answer*
> Ⓐ ● Ⓒ Ⓓ
>
> (A)   Every weekend
> (B)   The first two Wednesdays
> (C)   One afternoon a week
> (D)   Every other Wednesday

The reading selection says that the demonstrations are scheduled for the first and second Wednesdays of the month. Therefore, you should choose answer (B).

Now begin work on the questions.

Questions 161–162 refer to the following advertisement.

> You'll relax in our large, comfortable seats, with plenty of room to stretch. Complimentary headphones, magazines and books make your travel time entertaining and restful. You'll enjoy our award-winning service, beginning with your choice of beverage and snack, followed by a four-star meal and breathtaking dessert. Thanks to our Sister Company Program, you can fly to more than 600 cities in more than 120 countries. Purchase four, round-trip tickets, and your next domestic trip will be free. Go on, give us a call, and make your next trip a pleasurable one.

161. What is being advertised?

(A) A hotel chain
(B) A new restaurant
(C) An airline
(D) A shuttle service

162. What can the customer do after his fourth trip?

(A) Use the service in another country
(B) Pay nothing for travel within the country
(C) Visit any of the 600 cities
(D) Receive free accommodation

Questions 163–165 refer to the following notice.

In order to conserve electricity during these high-use months, the city government will implement its Save Now Plan on September 5 and 12. We are aiming for the same substantial savings that we saw last month and in July, when the plan debuted. Downtown area commercial businesses and residential owners are asked to follow the plan by stopping or reducing electricity use at the times detailed below. For additional plan details, call the City Information Hotline.

Type of Business	Time	Type of Consumption
Heavy Industry	1–5 p.m.	Lights, Industrial Applications
Light Industry	10 a.m.–2 p.m.	Air Conditioning, Lights
Office Buildings	9 a.m.–1 p.m.	Air Conditioning, Lights
Residences	10 a.m.–2 p.m.	Air Conditioning, Electrical Appliances
Retail Stores	2–6 p.m.	Air Conditioning, Lights

163. Who is not included in the Save Now Plan?

(A) Large companies
(B) Individually owned businesses and homeowners
(C) Factories and stores
(D) Hospitals

164. Why is the city implementing the plan?

(A) It has run out of electricity.
(B) It needs to save resources.
(C) It wants to attract new business.
(D) It has a surplus of energy.

165. How many times has the plan been used before?

(A) 0
(B) 1
(C) 2
(D) 3

GO ON TO THE NEXT PAGE

Memo

To: All Managers
From: Terry Lee
Re: Questionnaires
Date: April 11, 2002

Last week we distributed a short questionnaire to all employees. The purpose of this questionnaire is to determine the need for training. We recognize that employees have different levels of skill and knowledge concerning technology and software. With the completed surveys, we can more accurately assess the need for and type of training.

Please collect all questionnaires from your employees by April 15. Before giving them to my assistant, Charles, please make sure that none of your employees has included his or her name. It is very important that these remain anonymous.

By May 15, my department will release a findings report and proposal for training. If the proposal is approved, training programs will be recommended for certain employees.

---

166. What is the purpose of this memo?

(A) To explain what managers should do
(B) To cancel the program
(C) To determine the exact need for training
(D) To evaluate employees

167. How much time do the managers have to collect the questionnaires?

(A) As much time as they need
(B) More than a month
(C) Less than a week
(D) One more day

168. Who will receive training?

(A) Employees who include their names on the survey
(B) Everyone who needs it
(C) Employees who work with Charles
(D) Workers who received a recommendation

Questions 169–171 refer to the following article.

H URLEY MOTORCYCLES released a recall today for more than 2 million tires. Over the past year, three styles of tires are claimed to be responsible for 28 accidents, six including fatalities. In most cases, motorcycles driven at high speeds crashed when a tire, usually in the rear, blew up. The cause has not yet been determined, but experts believe that the tires have a faulty outside layer which may come off under high velocity or high heat conditions. Unlike most companies, Hurley manufactures and produces the tires for all Hurley models. Officials announced that they will immediately replace all affected tires.

169. What has been identified as part of the problem?

(A) Untrained drivers
(B) Velocity
(C) Poor bike design
(D) Tire installation

170. How many accidents were reported?

(A) 3
(B) 6
(C) More than 25
(D) It is unknown

171. What is Hurley planning to do for customers?

(A) Release a new motorcycle
(B) Exchange the tires
(C) Fix the old tires
(D) Stop manufacturing the product

Questions 172–173 refer to the following notice.

It is time to renew your insurance policy. In order to prepare your policy for the coming year, please contact a representative at the number listed. You will need to provide any changes to your address, the year and make of your vehicle(s), the approximate number of miles driven per year, and the current mileage. Please have this information available when you speak with a representative.

172. What information is **not** needed?

(A) Ages of all drivers
(B) Where the person lives
(C) How far the car is driven
(D) The type of car

173. How will the company gather the information?

(A) Through office visits
(B) Through postcards
(C) Through personal interviews
(D) Through phone calls

GO ON TO THE NEXT PAGE

Questions 174–176 refer to the following notice.

As a business and community leader, you are cordially invited to be our guest at the Richmond Reception for Small Business Leaders and Entrepreneurs. As you are aware, Richmond has experienced unprecedented growth in the last three years. Much of that growth is due to you and your business colleagues. The Richmond Small Business Network wants to take the opportunity to show its appreciation and begin working towards even greater development in the future.

The reception will be held at the historic Parisian Room of the Freemont Hotel. We will begin the festivities at 5:30 p.m. on October 11. Entertainment will be provided by The Jazz Ensemble. Light snacks and no-host bar.

Free parking is available at the Schooner Garage, located on the corner of Schooner and 5th Street. Please call 528-1213 for directions.

174. Who is invited to the reception?

(A) Hotel personnel
(B) Individual business people
(C) Multi-national representatives
(D) Former leaders

175. What word describes Richmond's recent economic growth?

(A) Slow
(B) Moderate
(C) Unusual
(D) Undocumented

176. What is **not** free?

(A) Attendance
(B) Parking
(C) Food
(D) Drinks

ALL PASSENGERS!

The Metropolitan Light Rail Authority has developed the following guidelines in the event of an emergency. For your safety, please read the following instructions.

- In all cases, wait for instructions from the train operator.

- Fire extinguishers and emergency service telephones are located at the end of each car. They can be removed by kicking in the plastic door panel.

- Never block doorways or aisles.

- In the event that you must exit the train, watch your step when exiting. If there is no electricity, doors can be opened by pulling apart from the middle. There is also an escape door on the roof of each car.

- Once you have left the train, look in both directions before crossing the tracks. Then, move away from the tracks to wait for a rescue train. Do not touch electrical rails.

Additional instructions are included on the back for assisting the elderly, infants and small children, and those passengers with disabilities.

---

177. For whom are the instructions written?

    (A) Bus riders
    (B) Pedestrians
    (C) Train passengers
    (D) Train operators

178. Where can phones be found?

    (A) In the conductor's car
    (B) In every car of the train
    (C) Near the escape door
    (D) Over the doors

179. What is the first thing that passengers should do in an emergency?

    (A) Leave the train
    (B) Telephone for assistance
    (C) Move articles from the aisle
    (D) Listen for instructions

180. What group are referred to in the instructions on the back?

    (A) Passengers who don't speak English
    (B) Railroad operators
    (C) All passengers
    (D) People over 70

GO ON TO THE NEXT PAGE

Audioview
1225 South Congress Avenue
Austin, TX 78701

August 7, 2001

Shana Lowry
Classic Clocks & Watches
1604 East 4th Street
Reno, NV 89507

Dear Ms. Lowry:

On May 1, I placed an order for 500 EF500 clocks to present to our top customers.

On May 15, I called Classic Clocks & Watches to check on the order. We were scheduled to begin distributing the clocks on June 15 and I wanted to confirm that we would have the clocks at our offices well in advance of that date. The customer service representative told me that she had no order from Audioview. I faxed a copy of the order to her and she told me that she would call me back with an answer. She never returned the call.

The clocks did not arrive until August 1. This customer service was the worst that I have ever experienced. I was given one excuse after another. My manager has lost confidence in my ability to complete a project. I can't tell you how disappointed I am with your company. The clocks were paid for in advance, so I can't tell you that I refuse to pay for them. Instead, I am asking for a substantial discount and refund. You may contact me at Audioview, 1-800-555-1456. I will call you if I have not heard from you by August 14.

Sincerely,

Nancy Iskander

181. What is the purpose of the letter?

(A) To make a complaint
(B) To praise a company
(C) To order some presents
(D) To discuss the customer service representatives

182. When did the merchandise arrive?

(A) On time
(B) More than two months after it was ordered
(C) Two weeks later than it was needed
(D) Three months ago

183. Why is Ms. Iskander so disappointed?

(A) She wanted to do a good job.
(B) The clocks weren't good quality.
(C) She lost her job.
(D) Ms. Lowry wasn't very helpful.

184. What does the writer want *Classic Clocks & Watches* to do?

(A) Return the payment
(B) Take the clocks back
(C) Give her additional clocks
(D) Pay back a portion of the total

Questions 185–186 refer to the following notice.

Attention Members

On Friday morning, March 2, the water will be shut off in the ladies' and men's locker rooms so that repairs can be made. The exact time will be posted on Thursday, March 1. We apologize for any inconvenience.

---

185. Where would this notice be seen?

(A) At a gym
(B) In a hospital
(C) In a dormitory
(D) At a hydroelectric plant

186. What will happen on March 1?

(A) The water will not work.
(B) The club will be closed.
(C) Members will be notified of the details.
(D) There will be no electricity.

Questions 187–188 refer to the following article.

SKYROCKETING PRICES for imported oil are threatening economies around the world. This was the message repeated at the trade ministers' quarterly meeting. While not wanting to alarm citizens and the business community, the politicians stressed that action taken now will avoid future problems. Price jumps of 30–40% over the last quarter have been seen around the region. Governments are pressuring the oil-producing nations to increase their output, thereby lowering the prices. Environmental groups sent representatives to encourage discussion on alternative sources of energy. The groups claim that long-term solutions will only result if countries place resources toward developing new solutions. Dependency on current energy sources will only result in recurring cycles of low and high prices. The outcome of the oil ministers' meeting scheduled for next week is greatly anticipated.

---

187. What is the problem?

(A) Oil spills in space
(B) Increased oil costs
(C) Oil producing nations won't comply with requests.
(D) Environmental groups protested.

188. What do the environmental groups claim?

(A) Different types of energy must be used.
(B) Increases of 35% are not bad.
(C) There is enough oil for everyone.
(D) Changes in energy prices cannot be stopped.

GO ON TO THE NEXT PAGE

Questions 189–190 refer to the following instructions.

Will the family farm become a thing of the past? That is exactly what we, Family Farmers United, are trying to avoid. Your contribution will go a long way. Our goal is to collect $1 million to help our members and to spread our message to the public. In past years, we have provided loans for struggling families, bought community machinery, and offered classes on agricultural technology. Ninety percent of the money collected goes toward programming and advocacy.

To make a donation, fill out the enclosed form. Indicate the amount that you would like to contribute. Mark the category that best describes your farm or situation. At the bottom of the form, please add any comments or ideas for future programs. We appreciate your support.

189. For whom are the instructions written?

(A) Agriculture engineers
(B) Large farming companies
(C) Lawmakers
(D) Individual farmers

190. How is the money used?

(A) To assist farmers who need help
(B) To record the history of farming
(C) To buy new farms
(D) To create a radio program

Questions 191–193 refer to the following letter.

Nikolo-Yamskaya, d.6
109189 Moscow, Russia

March 21, 2000

Bob Jenkins
At Your Service
5500 Connecticut Avenue, NW, Suite 204
Washington, D.C., 20009

Dear Mr. Jenkins:

Please let me thank you for all your help. I contacted your company last year when I had to plan a trip for the president of the company where I work, Moscow Express. Moscow Express is the top travel agency in Moscow and we are very proud of the service that we provide for our clients. When our president had to go to Washington for meetings, I knew that he expected outstanding service. I spent 10 years in California but am not very familiar with the east coast. That was the reason that I wanted to work with a travel agency in the United States. Some of my Russian colleagues recommended At Your Service.

I was nervous because I wanted the trip to be absolutely perfect for Mr. Kritschnev. There was no reason to be worried. The first thing that Mr. Kritschnev did when he returned to Moscow was to come to my office and praise me for the trip! Thank you so much! He said that it was the best planned trip of his career and that the service was more than he ever expected.

He even took notes so that we could try to offer the same type of service here in Russia. I now handle all of Mr. Kritschnev's trips and I owe it all to you. Thank you again for all of your help. If you are ever in Moscow, please let me know so that we can show you around our beautiful city.

Sincerely,

Dova Krugov

Dova Krugov
Travel Planner
Moscow Express

---

191. What did Mr. Jenkins do?

(A) Worked with Dova to arrange a trip
(B) Went to Moscow to meet Mr. Kritschnev
(C) Created a bad impression
(D) Competed with Moscow Express

192. Where did Dova Krugov live for a decade?

(A) In Washington, D.C.
(B) In California
(C) In Moscow
(D) On the east coast

193. What happened as a result of Mr. Kritschnev's trip?

(A) Ms. Krugov toured Washington, D.C.
(B) Mr. Jenkins was invited to Moscow
(C) Dova exclusively arranges the president's travel
(D) At Your Service was fired

GO ON TO THE NEXT PAGE

Questions 194–195 refer to the following notice.

TELEPHONE SERVICE OFFER!

Sign up now for our long distance service and receive free activation. That's right, no charge! Our connection gives you single or multiple lines for one, low price. Today, more than ever, an extra line is a necessity, not a luxury. Don't pay more with other companies, when you can choose up to three lines for the same price. It's easy!

194. What item is being offered at no charge?

(A) Local service
(B) One line
(C) Multiple lines
(D) Start-up

195. How are multiple lines described?

(A) Needed
(B) Extravagant
(C) Costly
(D) Hard to get

Questions 196–197 refer to the following article.

The Wingnut Fly, native of several Central American countries, has been spotted in Riverside County. The fly is known to carry a virus deadly to numerous species of vegetables. County officials released a report yesterday and called an emergency meeting.

The last time the fly was spotted in this agricultural region, it caused more than $1.5 million in damage. Officials say that swift action is needed to eradicate the fly before it multiplies and spreads to other areas. They have called in experts and have alerted farmers. An emergency hotline telephone number is being established.

196. What is known about the fly?

(A) It can cause great harm to crops.
(B) It has a short lifespan.
(C) It has never appeared before in the region.
(D) It is native to the area.

197. What step has **not** been taken?

(A) A special meeting was held.
(B) Vegetable growers were told.
(C) Pesticides have been sprayed.
(D) Specialists are working on the problem.

Cann, Donovan and Tout
8 High Street
Dublin, Ireland

Travessa do Salitre, 7
1206-066 Lisbon, Portugal

Dear Mr. Gacche:

It is my pleasure to offer you the job of Marketing Director for Cann, Donovan and Tout. Our agency takes its time to search for and find the most talented candidates. We are sure that you will be glad to join such an elite group. Attached is a letter of understanding regarding the position. Please read it over, sign and return to Angelica Toullez at the address indicated.

As we discussed, you will begin on October 2 and will spend the first month training and visiting our various offices. We have arranged a preliminary schedule of visits:

October 9–11	Bonn
October 19–20	Brussels
October 23–24	Barcelona
October 30–31	Brighton

Our travel coordinator, Sheila Dunn, will make hotel and flight arrangements. If you have preferences for airlines or hotels, please contact her.

According to the terms of your employment, we will provide you with a car. Enclosed is a list of five car models from which you should choose. Albert Garcia can assist you with the details of the car, insurance, and paperwork, once you have made your choice.

If you have any questions or need any information, feel free to contact Barbara Lau, Vice President of Marketing. You will report directly to her. Once again, congratulations on your choice of Cann, Donovan and Tout. Enclosed you will find a check for the signing bonus.

Sincerely,

Matt Cann
Principal

---

198. What is the purpose of the letter?

(A) To promote Cann, Donovan and Tout
(B) To arrange a job interview
(C) To accept a job offer
(D) To offer Mr. Gacche a new position

199. Which of the following is **not** included in the letter?

(A) Money for accepting the job
(B) Automobile information
(C) Directions to the office
(D) A schedule of visits

200. Who should Mr. Gacche call if he has questions regarding his daily work?

(A) Ms. Dunn
(B) Mr. Cann
(C) Ms. Lau
(D) Mr. Garcia

Stop! This is the end of the test. If you finish before one hour and fifteen minutes have passed, you may go back to Parts V, VI, and VII and check your work.

Grammar Glossary

Adjectives

Adjectives are words that describe a noun. In English they do not change to match gender, case, or number.

    (adj) *(adj)*   *(adj)*
The *large, brown* box is on the *file* cabinet.

Adjectives: Descriptive Phrases

Descriptive adjectives describe a quality or a state of a noun. Several types of phrases can serve as adjectives.

Participle phrase

The manager *waiting by the door near the window* is …

Prepositional phrase

The manager *by the desk near the window* is …

Infinitive phrase

The only manager *to get a promotion* is …

Adjectives: Determiners

A determiner is a word that is used with a noun to limit its meaning in some way. The following classes of words can be used as determiners:

Articles

the, a, an

  A letter was put on *the* desk near *the* window.

Demonstrative adjectives

Single   *this that*
Plural   *these those*

  This letter was addressed to the lawyer who was out of town.
  Can you see *those* people over there?

Possessive adjectives

Pronouns   *my, one's, his, her, its, our, their*
Nouns   *Kim's, the manager's*

  My office is next to the *President's* office.

Numerals

Cardinal   *one, two, three*
Ordinal   *first, second, third*

  The *third* time you are late you will lose one day's pay.

Indefinite quantity

more, most, some, few, any

  We stayed *most* of the night working on a few projects.

Adverbs

Adverbs modify verbs and adjectives. They are used to describe how something happens or to modify an adjective.

Adverbs are often formed by adding *-ly* to an adjective.

rare / rarely, slow / slowly, easy / easily, final / finally, careful / carefully, careless / carelessly, quiet / quietly, beautiful / beautifully, heavy / heavily

To say how something happens
  She *quickly* learned to photocopy.
  She learned *quickly* to photocopy.

  Anna *slowly* got used to her new job.
  Anna got used to her new job *slowly*.

To modify an adjective
  Mike is *incredibly* pleased with his promotion.
  Rafi is *extremely* good at his job.

Position of adverbs

Before or after the subject
  Occasionally David comes to the office late.
  We *sometimes* allow our clients to roll over their accounts for 90 days.
  Generally they pay us on time.

Before the verb or adjective
  He is *usually* early on Fridays.
  David *occasionally* comes to work after 9:00 a.m.
  Our clients *generally* pay us on time.

Following the verb *be*
  Eric is *frequently* the first to arrive; he is *nearly* always here before 8:00a.m.
  The new CEO is *finally* coming to terms with the union's requests.

Between the auxiliary (helping verb or modal) and the main verb
> The shareholder's meeting has *traditionally* been held in August.
> Our marketing division could *probably* take on more territory in the New Year.

Following the subject in questions
> Does the accounts department *ever* allow employees to have a salary advance?
> Will the management *finally* get new furniture in the cafeteria?

Adverbs: Date/Time/Sequence Markers

Date, time, and sequence markers are used to tell when an event occurred.

Date markers
on, by, since, from ... to, before

> I'll meet you in Seoul *on* the fifteenth of August.
> I should arrive in London *by* the 26th of this month.
> We've been in Milan *since* September 23rd.
> I'm going to be in Riyadh *from* April 9th *to* April 12th.
> The report should be complete *before* the end of the week.

Time markers
before, after, when, since, as soon as, by the time that ...

> *Before* I open the meeting I would like to thank Mr. Park for changing his plans.
> He said he would deal with it *after* he had made a few urgent phone calls.
> *When* the time is right we'll put in an offer – but not before.
> A great deal has happened *since* the last meeting.
> I'll get on with the main point *as soon as* we have heard the minutes from the shareholders meeting.
> *By the time that* we arrive in Paris, the new program should be in place.

Sequence markers
first, first of all, to begin with
second, secondly, then, subsequently, later
finally, to conclude, in conclusion, in the end

> *First*, I would like to talk about our new program. *Then* I will tell you about the effects of the take-over. *To conclude* I will address the challenges we face in the coming year.

Adverbs: Frequency Words

Adverbs of frequency are used to discuss how often an action or event takes place. Common adverbs of frequency are:

always, nearly always, often, usually, sometimes, occasionally, rarely, hardly ever, never

> We *always* lock the office when we leave at night.
> She *nearly always* brings her lunch to work.
> Maria *often* eats her lunch in the park, with Yoshi.
> The company *usually* allows customers to visit the factory.
> Groups of school children *sometimes* visit the offices.
> The management *occasionally* buys lunch for everyone.
> They *rarely* spend more than $5.00 on each employee.
> Ms. Tamura *hardly ever* drives to work; she usually walks.
> Mr. Sanchez *never* arrives late to work.

Adverbs of frequency can also be used to discuss regular occurrences. Common adverbs used for this purpose are:

weekly, every day, every other day, yearly/annually

> Our *weekly* meetings take place every Tuesday.
> We have departmental meetings every day.
> There are progress meetings *every other day*; on Monday, Wednesday and Friday.
> Mr. Sung Park visits Seoul annually.

Cause and Effect

Cause and effect sentences indicate what happened (the effect) and why it happend (the cause).
In a cause and effect sentence, either the cause or the effect clause or phrase can begin the sentence:

>   (*cause*)   (*effect*)
> The downturn in the economy has upset our expansion plans.

(effect)   *(cause)*
Our expansion plans have been upset by the downturn in
the economy.

Some common words that introduce a clause of cause
or reason are:
*since, as, because, because of, due to, on account of,
out of, from*

       (effect)   *(cause)*
    We missed the start of the meeting, *on account of* us
    being late.

Some common words that indicate an effect or result are:
*so that, so, as a result, therefore, consequently, thus,
resulted from, caused*

       (cause)   *(effect)*
    We were late for the conference and *as a result* we did
    not hear the plenary.

Clauses: Main and Subordinate Clauses

A main clause, also called an independent clause, is a
complete sentence and can stand by itself.

    (Subject) (Verb)
    She   worked until ten o'clock.

A sentence may include more than one main clause. A
sentence with two main clauses is joined by a
conjunction. A comma is generally used between the
clauses.

    The meeting started at 1:00p.m., but Erin didn't arrive
    until 1:30p.m.

A subordinate, or dependent clause, cannot stand by
itself. It depends on the main clause of the sentence.

    If you need help, *give me a call.*

Comparatives and Superlatives

Comparatives
The ending *-er* and the word *than* are used to identify the
comparative. This form is used to compare one person,
thing, action or group with another person, thing, action
or group.

    His computer is *faster than* my computer.

Sometimes, the second item is not mentioned because
it is understood by the audience.

    His computer is *faster.*

Superlatives
The article *the* followed by an adjective with the ending
-est indicates the superlative. This form is used to
compare one person, thing, etc. with a whole group.

    Of all the sales divisions, our division brought in *the
    largest* revenues.

Often these compared things are understood and are not
written.

    Our division brought in *the largest* revenues.

Conditionals

Conditionals are used to describe hypothetical cause
and effect situations. There are three common types of
conditionals: real future possibility, present unreal, and
past unreal.

Real future possibility
If + present simple   *will* + base form
(Hypothetical cause)   *(possible effect)*

    If I have time, I will finish the report tomorrow morning.
    He will arrive at 9:00p.m. if he catches the 2:00p.m.
    flight.

Present unreal possibility
If + simple past   would + base form
(Hypothetical cause)   *(possible effect)*

    If I were promoted today, I would go to the London office.
    I would send him a catalogue if I had his address.

Past unreal possibility
If + have + past participle   would + have + past
                          participle
(Hypothetical cause)   *(possible effect)*

This conditional is often used to express REGRET or
RELIEF about things that have never happened, which
could either have consequences in the present or had
consequences in the past.

Regret
    If she had worked harder, she would have passed the
    exam.
    We would have bought a bigger computer if we had had
    more money.

Relief
    We wouldn't have survived if the bank hadn't lent us
    the money.
    If I hadn't arrived late, I would never have met the new
    CEO.

Conditional: *should / would*

Should and *would* are sometimes referred to as the conditional in sentences such as:

I should like to attend the conference in Saudi Arabia next year.
I would join you in Penang for the meeting.

The condition *if* is implied in these structures.

I should like to attend the conference in Saudi Arabia next year (if I can find the time).
I would join you in Penang for the meeting (if I could, but I can't get away).

Conjunctions

Conjunctions are words that are used to join words, phrases or clauses to show relationships between ideas.

Common conjunctions are:
and, but, yet, or, nor, so

Paired conjunctions are:
not only ... but also, both ... and, either ... or, neither ... nor

Addition
Tom usually goes to the cafe next door for lunch, *and* so do I.
I like *not only* your methods, *but also* your presentation.

Contrast
We want to open a Moscow office, *but* it would be too expensive.
He can't open a simple computer file, *yet* he talks like an expert.

Alternative
We have to decide if we are going to open a branch in Los Angeles *or* Boston.
We are not going to the conference in Sydney, *nor* are we going to Paris this year.

Choice
We will promote *either* Mohammed *or* Philip to the management position, but not both.
You can take *either* Friday afternoon *or* Monday morning off.

Negative choice
Neither the administration department *nor* the maintenance department will benefit from the changes in management.
I would *not* recommend *either* candidate for the position.

Result
We needed a lot more production space, *so* we opened a new facility in New Zealand.
We added more employees, *so* we needed more space.

Gerunds and Infinitives

Gerunds
Gerunds are formed by adding *-ing* to the simple form of the verb. They are used in the following ways:

Subject nouns
Working for this company is very rewarding.

Object nouns
Most of our employees enjoy *working* here.

As the object of a preposition
Mr. Susumura is very happy *about transferring* to Washington DC.

Following the preposition *to*
We are looking forward *to meeting* you.

Many verbs and phrases are usually followed only by gerunds. These include:
admit, consider, deny, excuse, finish, involve, postpone, quit, regret, suggest, to keep on, there's no point in, to have difficulty.

Infinitives
Infinitives are formed by adding *to* to the base form of the verb. They are used in the following ways:

Following select verbs.
hope to, plan to, agree to, offer to, expect to, refuse to, need to

We *offered to redo* the proposal.

Following select verbs + noun/pronoun
tell someone to, invite someone to, allow someone to, warn someone to, would like someone to, need someone to, encourage someone to

I *would like you to back-up* your files before you turn off your computer.

Many verbs and phrases are **usually** followed only by infinitives. These include:
agree, arrange, ask, care, claim, consent, decide, demand

We *decided to outsource* all of our accounting functions.

Some verbs and phrases can be followed **only** by infinitives. These include:
begin, can't stand, continue, neglect, propose, try

We *tried to reach* you by phone this morning.

See a standard grammar text for extended lists of verbs to use with gerunds and infinitives.

Nouns: Count/Non-count

Count nouns refer to things that can be counted. They are expressed as either singular or plural.

computer/computers, employee/employees, office / offices, worker/workers, file/files, machine/machines, fax/faxes

Non-count nouns refer to things that cannot usually be counted.

machinery, food, water, love, work, training, homework, business, information, research, advice, news

Articles with count nouns
Singular count nouns take *a/an*.

I need *a* new computer.
The meeting is being held in *an* office in Sydney.

Plural count nouns take *some/any*.

Are there *any* workers in the dispatch office today?
I came to see if I could get *some* faxes sent out today.

Plural count nouns also take *many* and *a few*.

Our company doesn't have *many* employees.
There are only *a few* companies like ours in Thailand.

Articles with non-count nouns
Non-count nouns don't generally take *a/an*. Some of the articles used with non-count nouns are: *much, a little, a great deal of, a lot ... of* and *lots of*.

Unfortunately, we didn't get *much* work done today.
I'll ask him if he could spend *a little* time on this job.
We have *a great deal of* information on their activities.
He's going to need *a lot of* training for this work.
She requires *lots of* advice on this matter.

Nouns: Singular/Plural

Most nouns (words that name objects/places/people) are regular. The plural of regular nouns is formed by adding *-s* to the base form.

office/offices, employee/employees, file/files, desk/desks, car/cars

However, some English nouns are irregular. They have to be changed significantly to form the plural.

man/men, mouse/mice, tooth/teeth

See a standard grammar text for extended lists of irregular nouns.

Nouns: Suffixes *-er, -or, -ist*

The suffixes *-er* and *-or* usually indicate a person who carries out a task or vocation.

plumber, firefighter, engineer, carpenter, (police) officer, astronomer, writer, driver, doctor, ambassador, actor

A *firefighter* is a person who fights fires.
A *driver* is a person who drives.

The suffix *-ist* modifies a word so that it refers to a member of a group or occupation (often of an artistic or scientific nature).

economist, physiologist, psychologist, artist, anesthesiologist, scientist

An *economist* is someone who specializes in economy.
A *psychologist* is someone who specializes in psychology.

Parallel Structures

Parallel structures are sentences containing two or more structures that share the same grammatical function, joined by an appropriate conjunction.

Parallel past simple
He *called* the waiter and *asked* for the check.

Parallel adjectives
She's *young* and *inexperienced*, but I think she'll work out.

Parallel infinitives
We have managed *to control* spending, *resist* excessive hiring, and *avoid* laying-off too many people.

Parallel gerunds
He enjoys *cycling*, *playing* tennis, and *walking* in his spare time.

Participles *-ed/-ing*

The present participle (*-ing*)
The present participle is formed by adding *-ing* to the base form of the verb. In addition to being used to form the progressive tense, the present participle functions as a gerund and as an adjective.

We *are buying* stock in the high-tech markets.
Buying stock can be very risky.
The *smiling* broker dealt with my request.

Past participle (*-ed*)
The past participle is formed by adding *-ed* to the base form of regular verbs.

We had *placed* the order too late.

Irregular verbs use a variety of endings.

The bank has *lent* us the money.
She will have *taught* the new employees the procedures by next week.

See a standard grammar text for extended lists of irregular verbs.

In addition to being used to form the perfect simple tenses (past, present and future), the past participle is used with *to be* to form the passive.

Our computers *were programmed* to shut down at midnight on Friday.

Parts of Speech

Nouns
Words that name people, objects and places.
man, John, desk, paper, office, hospital, Paris, Belgium

Verbs
Words that name actions, feelings and events.
walk, run, photocopy, negotiate, work, drive

Adjectives
Words that describe nouns.
a beautiful car, a lovely day, a wonderful report

Adverbs
Words that describe the action of verbs.
He ran quickly. They happily signed the contract.

Pronouns
Words that are used in the place of nouns.
he, she, it, they
his, her, its, their

Mrs. Jones works here. *She* works here.
The report is Mrs. Jones' work. *It* is *her* work.

Comparatives/Superlatives
Words that modify adjectives

fast/faster/the fastest
expensive/more expensive/the most expensive

Conjunctions
Words and phrases that join clauses

and, so, but, for, and yet, so that,
nevertheless, or, that, unless

Prepositions
Words and phrases that talk about time, location, possession, and direction

before this, *next to* the storeroom,
the leg *of* the chair, *to* the bank.

Articles
Words that indicate whether a noun is definite or indefinite
Definite (*the*)
  The man over there is my boss.
Indefinite (*a/an*)
  Would you give me a pencil, please?
Zero article
  __ Cats are not allowed at __ work.
Zero article is used with certain plural nouns or nouns that do not need an article.

Prefixes and Suffixes

Prefixes
Prefixes are groups of letters added to the beginning of base words that change the function or meaning of the word.

*dis*like, *de*centralize, *mis*manage, *super*market, *out*bid, *pro*-government, *inter*national, *post*script, *multi*cultural, *auto*biographical, *proto*type, *vice*-president, *semi*annual

Prefixes usually do not change the grammatical function of a word. Verbs remain verbs; nouns remain nouns, etc.

Suffixes
Suffixes are groups of letters added to the end of base words that change the function or meaning of the word.

London*er*, wait*er*/wait*ress* (gender based), book*let*, brother*hood*, scholar*ship*, refin*ery*, grate*ful*, Malays*ian*, Yemen*i*, Japan*ese*, socia*lite*, socia*list*, idea*lism*, organiz*ation*, centr*al*, sad*ness*, qual*ify*, worth*less*

Suffixes can change the grammatical function of a word. Verbs can become nouns or adjectives; nouns can become adjectives, etc.

See a standard grammar text for extended lists of prefixes and suffixes.

Prepositions: Objects

The prepositional object is the noun phrase following a preposition.

	Prep.	Prep. Object
His lateness only added	*to*	*the problem.*
Has the Board responded	*to*	*their demands?*
We really hope to build	*on*	*our success.*
Our creditors have asked	*for*	*help.*

Prepositional Phrases with *by*

Prepositional phrases with *by* indicate
  means (how?)
  time (when?)
  position (where?)
  agent (by whom?)

Means
  He arrived *by plane* from Brussels.
  (Explains how he arrived.)
  By signing this contract we have doubled our holdings.
  (Explains how have we doubled our holdings.)

Time
  By the time he arrived the work was finished.
  (Explains when the work was finished.)

Position
  She was *by the CEO* in the picture.
  (Explains where she was standing.)

Agent
  This report was written *by the Research Department*.
  (Explains who wrote the report.)

Prepositions of Location

These are generally used to describe the position of two or more objects, relative to each other.

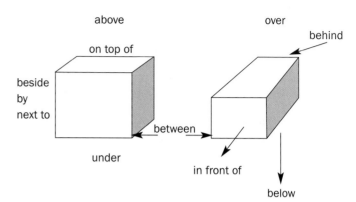

The visitors' parking lot is *between* the warehouse and the main office.
There's a pay phone *next to* the warehouse.
I'll meet you *by* the coke machine in front of the warehouse.
The employees' parking lot is two floors *below* the main office building.
There's a helicopter pad *on top of* the warehouse.
We can store this stuff *behind* the warehouse until we need it.
Is there any storage *in* the basement *under* the warehouse?
There's a sign *above* the warehouse.
We are worried about the planes passing *over* the main office building.
People usually smoke near the tables *beside* the main office building.
Our visitors park *in front of* the building.

Pronouns

Pronouns are used in place of nouns. There are three basic types of pronoun: subject pronouns, object pronouns and possessive pronouns. They can be singular or plural.

Subject pronouns
I, you, he, she, it we, you, they

  I read your report; *it* was very good

Object pronouns
me, you, him, her, it, us, you, them

  They want to meet *us* on Friday morning.

Possessive pronouns
mine, yours, hers, his, its ours, yours, theirs

  Is this your coffee or *hers*?

Quantity Words

some, any, all, a few, a little, a lot of, a great deal, not many, not much

See Nouns: Count/non-count for more on quantity words

Subject: Redundant Subject

A sentence or a clause only has one subject. You cannot have two subjects.

Incorrect: There's a man in reception *who he* says he has an appointment.
Correct: There's a man in reception *who* says he has an appointment.

Incorrect: We have a new facility in Rome *that it* will double our productivity.
Correct: We have a new facility in Rome *that* will double our productivity.

Incorrect: Their new office, *which it* is in Colombo, is really beautiful.
Correct: Their new office, *which* is in Colombo, is really beautiful.

Subject and Verbs of Sentence

All sentences in English must contain a subject and a verb.
In English the subject is usually the noun, pronoun or noun phrase that is the focus of the sentence. The predicate is the rest of the sentence, and contains the verb and object.

(*subject*)	(*predicate*)
Our latest acquisition	has been a real asset to our holdings.
Mario and Tina both	work in the Research and Development Department.

The subject determines the agreement of the sentence. (See Verb agreement)
In English the verb is part of the predicate and refers to the actions carried out by the subject.

	(*verb*)
Our latest acquisition	*has been* a real asset to our holdings.
Mario and Tina	*work* in the Research and Development Department.
They	*have been working* there for 2 years.

Synonyms

Synonyms are words or phrases that have similar meanings to other words.

place of work = *office, headquarters, agency, bureau*
hardworking = *assiduous, diligent, industrious*

Verbs: Active/Passive

There are two ways to express information in sentences that use transitive verbs (verbs that can have objects) – active and passive.

Active

In an active sentence the subject is responsible for the action; the object of the sentence is the recipient of the action. The subject (sometimes called the agent) is the focus in an active sentence.

(*subject/agent*)	(*active verb*)	(*object/recipient*)
The manager	purchased	the new software.
The Federal Reserve	lowered	the interest rate.

Passive

In a passive sentence the recipient of the action is the subject. The verb becomes passive by using the appropriate auxiliary verb and the past participle of the verb. The action is the focus in a passive sentence, not the agent.

(*recipient*)	(*passive verb*)	(*optional agent*)
The new software	was purchased	by the manager.
The interest rate	was lowered	by the Federal Reserve.

Verbs: Stative

Stative verbs are verbs that are normally not used in the progressive tense (see Verb Tenses). They are often verbs of emotion or verbs that refer to ideas that do not change:

Verbs of senses
  see, hear, feel, taste, smell
Verbs of emotion
  love, hate, like, differ, desire
Verbs of perception
  believe, know, understand, remember
Verbs of measurement
  cost, equal, measure, weigh
Verbs of relationship
  belong, contain, have, own

Correct	Incorrect
I *love* working here.	I *am loving* working here.
My opinion *differs* from yours.	My opinion *is differing* from yours.

I *believe* you are correct.   I *am believing* you are correct.

We *own* that office block   We *are owning* that office block.

Also we normally use *have* in a stative manner when it is being used to describe possession.

Correct	Incorrect
I *have* a cold.	I *am having* a cold.
She *has* a new car.	She *is having* a new car.

Verb Agreement

The subject/verb must always agree in number. A singular noun takes a singular verb form and a plural noun takes a plural verb form.

Singular Subject	Verb
Our chief accountant	*lives* about twenty miles from the office.
An MA with five years work experience	*is* needed for this position.

Plural Subject	Verb
Most of our employees	*live* in the suburbs.
An MA and five years work experience	*are* needed for this position.

The subject and the verb must always agree, even if separated.

Separated by preposition
  Most of the ideas put forward by your department *are* good.
  The diagram on page sixteen in this training handbook *is* very good.

Separated by clause
  A lot of the things that I really love *were* in that suitcase.
  The number of people who came late today *is* very high.

Gerunds always take a singular verb
  Training our employees *is* an important part of our program.
  Smoking in the workplace *is* not allowed.

Verb Tenses

There are three time frames in the English tense system: present, past and future.

There are two simple tenses – present and past. The future is expressed using combinations of *will/shall* and *going to*. These three tenses can be expressed as either: simple, progressive, perfect or perfect progressive.

Present time frame
Simple Present
  She *checks* her e-mail every morning.
Present Progressive
  She *is checking* her e-mail at the moment.
Present Perfect
  She *has* already *checked* her e-mail.
Present Perfect Progressive
  She *has been checking* her e-mail since 9:30 a.m.

Past time frame
Simple Past
  She *checked* her e-mail at 6:30 last night.
Past Progressive
  She *was checking* her e-mail when the alarm rang.
Past Perfect
  She *had checked* her e-mail before I arrived.
Past Perfect Progressive
  She *had been checking* her e-mail all morning and felt tired.

Future time frame
Future Simple
  She *will check* her e-mail when she comes in.
Future Progressive
  She *will be checking* her e-mail when we arrive.
Future Perfect
  She *will have checked* her e-mail by 10:30 a.m.
Future Perfect Progressive
  She *will have been checking* her e-mail for 2 hours by the time we arrive.

To discuss future events we can also use *going to*, the simple present and present progressive.

going to Future
  She *is going to check* her e-mail before she leaves.
going to be + ing
  She *is going to be checking* her e-mail when we arrive.
Simple Present
  My plane *leaves* Boston at 7:00, and arrives in Washington at 8:30.
Present Progressive
  I *am meeting* my new boss at 8:45 tomorrow.

Verb + Prepositions

Verbs often form partnerships with prepositions, called phrasal verbs. Many of these partnerships are idiomatic. The combined verb + preposition may have a meaning that differs from the meaning of the verb alone. The meaning can often be worked out from the context:

The presenter *enlarged* on the topic during question time.
Will he *run for* President next year?

Verb + preposition partnerships can be separable or non-separable. The meaning of the phrasal verb often changes.

Separable
The credit card company *called* him *up* about his debts.

Non-separable
The government *has called up* reserve troops because of this emergency.

Word Families

Word families are groups of words that have a common base word. Most word families consist of noun, verb, adjective and adverb.

Noun	photograph	exclusion
Verb	to photograph	to exclude
Adjective	photographic	exclusive
Adverb	photographically	exclusively

Noun	Look at *the photographs* of the new product.
Verb	We need *to photograph* the damage to the shipment.
Adjective	Our insurers want us to get a *photographic* record.
Adverb	We'll keep the evidence *photographically*.

Noun	We need to maintain an *exclusion* area around our research area.
Verb	Our competitors were *excluded* from the invitation.
Adjective	We have a very *exclusive* clientele.
Adverb	We deal *exclusively* with the international community.

Answer Sheet Practice Test 1

Listening Comprehension

Part I
1 Ⓐ Ⓑ Ⓒ Ⓓ
2 Ⓐ Ⓑ Ⓒ Ⓓ
3 Ⓐ Ⓑ Ⓒ Ⓓ
4 Ⓐ Ⓑ Ⓒ Ⓓ
5 Ⓐ Ⓑ Ⓒ Ⓓ
6 Ⓐ Ⓑ Ⓒ Ⓓ
7 Ⓐ Ⓑ Ⓒ Ⓓ
8 Ⓐ Ⓑ Ⓒ Ⓓ
9 Ⓐ Ⓑ Ⓒ Ⓓ
10 Ⓐ Ⓑ Ⓒ Ⓓ
11 Ⓐ Ⓑ Ⓒ Ⓓ
12 Ⓐ Ⓑ Ⓒ Ⓓ
13 Ⓐ Ⓑ Ⓒ Ⓓ
14 Ⓐ Ⓑ Ⓒ Ⓓ
15 Ⓐ Ⓑ Ⓒ Ⓓ
16 Ⓐ Ⓑ Ⓒ Ⓓ
17 Ⓐ Ⓑ Ⓒ Ⓓ
18 Ⓐ Ⓑ Ⓒ Ⓓ
19 Ⓐ Ⓑ Ⓒ Ⓓ
20 Ⓐ Ⓑ Ⓒ Ⓓ

Part II
21 Ⓐ Ⓑ Ⓒ
22 Ⓐ Ⓑ Ⓒ
23 Ⓐ Ⓑ Ⓒ
24 Ⓐ Ⓑ Ⓒ
25 Ⓐ Ⓑ Ⓒ
26 Ⓐ Ⓑ Ⓒ
27 Ⓐ Ⓑ Ⓒ
28 Ⓐ Ⓑ Ⓒ
29 Ⓐ Ⓑ Ⓒ
30 Ⓐ Ⓑ Ⓒ
31 Ⓐ Ⓑ Ⓒ
32 Ⓐ Ⓑ Ⓒ
33 Ⓐ Ⓑ Ⓒ
34 Ⓐ Ⓑ Ⓒ
35 Ⓐ Ⓑ Ⓒ
36 Ⓐ Ⓑ Ⓒ
37 Ⓐ Ⓑ Ⓒ
38 Ⓐ Ⓑ Ⓒ
39 Ⓐ Ⓑ Ⓒ
40 Ⓐ Ⓑ Ⓒ
41 Ⓐ Ⓑ Ⓒ
42 Ⓐ Ⓑ Ⓒ
43 Ⓐ Ⓑ Ⓒ
44 Ⓐ Ⓑ Ⓒ
45 Ⓐ Ⓑ Ⓒ
46 Ⓐ Ⓑ Ⓒ
47 Ⓐ Ⓑ Ⓒ
48 Ⓐ Ⓑ Ⓒ
49 Ⓐ Ⓑ Ⓒ
50 Ⓐ Ⓑ Ⓒ

Part III
51 Ⓐ Ⓑ Ⓒ Ⓓ
52 Ⓐ Ⓑ Ⓒ Ⓓ
53 Ⓐ Ⓑ Ⓒ Ⓓ
54 Ⓐ Ⓑ Ⓒ Ⓓ
55 Ⓐ Ⓑ Ⓒ Ⓓ
56 Ⓐ Ⓑ Ⓒ Ⓓ
57 Ⓐ Ⓑ Ⓒ Ⓓ
58 Ⓐ Ⓑ Ⓒ Ⓓ
59 Ⓐ Ⓑ Ⓒ Ⓓ
60 Ⓐ Ⓑ Ⓒ Ⓓ
61 Ⓐ Ⓑ Ⓒ Ⓓ
62 Ⓐ Ⓑ Ⓒ Ⓓ
63 Ⓐ Ⓑ Ⓒ Ⓓ
64 Ⓐ Ⓑ Ⓒ Ⓓ
65 Ⓐ Ⓑ Ⓒ Ⓓ
66 Ⓐ Ⓑ Ⓒ Ⓓ
67 Ⓐ Ⓑ Ⓒ Ⓓ
68 Ⓐ Ⓑ Ⓒ Ⓓ
69 Ⓐ Ⓑ Ⓒ Ⓓ
70 Ⓐ Ⓑ Ⓒ Ⓓ
71 Ⓐ Ⓑ Ⓒ Ⓓ
72 Ⓐ Ⓑ Ⓒ Ⓓ
73 Ⓐ Ⓑ Ⓒ Ⓓ
74 Ⓐ Ⓑ Ⓒ Ⓓ
75 Ⓐ Ⓑ Ⓒ Ⓓ
76 Ⓐ Ⓑ Ⓒ Ⓓ
77 Ⓐ Ⓑ Ⓒ Ⓓ
78 Ⓐ Ⓑ Ⓒ Ⓓ
79 Ⓐ Ⓑ Ⓒ Ⓓ
80 Ⓐ Ⓑ Ⓒ Ⓓ

Part IV
81 Ⓐ Ⓑ Ⓒ Ⓓ
82 Ⓐ Ⓑ Ⓒ Ⓓ
83 Ⓐ Ⓑ Ⓒ Ⓓ
84 Ⓐ Ⓑ Ⓒ Ⓓ
85 Ⓐ Ⓑ Ⓒ Ⓓ
86 Ⓐ Ⓑ Ⓒ Ⓓ
87 Ⓐ Ⓑ Ⓒ Ⓓ
88 Ⓐ Ⓑ Ⓒ Ⓓ
89 Ⓐ Ⓑ Ⓒ Ⓓ
90 Ⓐ Ⓑ Ⓒ Ⓓ
91 Ⓐ Ⓑ Ⓒ Ⓓ
92 Ⓐ Ⓑ Ⓒ Ⓓ
93 Ⓐ Ⓑ Ⓒ Ⓓ
94 Ⓐ Ⓑ Ⓒ Ⓓ
95 Ⓐ Ⓑ Ⓒ Ⓓ
96 Ⓐ Ⓑ Ⓒ Ⓓ
97 Ⓐ Ⓑ Ⓒ Ⓓ
98 Ⓐ Ⓑ Ⓒ Ⓓ
99 Ⓐ Ⓑ Ⓒ Ⓓ
100 Ⓐ Ⓑ Ⓒ Ⓓ

Reading

Part V
101 Ⓐ Ⓑ Ⓒ Ⓓ
102 Ⓐ Ⓑ Ⓒ Ⓓ
103 Ⓐ Ⓑ Ⓒ Ⓓ
104 Ⓐ Ⓑ Ⓒ Ⓓ
105 Ⓐ Ⓑ Ⓒ Ⓓ
106 Ⓐ Ⓑ Ⓒ Ⓓ
107 Ⓐ Ⓑ Ⓒ Ⓓ
108 Ⓐ Ⓑ Ⓒ Ⓓ
109 Ⓐ Ⓑ Ⓒ Ⓓ
110 Ⓐ Ⓑ Ⓒ Ⓓ
111 Ⓐ Ⓑ Ⓒ Ⓓ
112 Ⓐ Ⓑ Ⓒ Ⓓ
113 Ⓐ Ⓑ Ⓒ Ⓓ
114 Ⓐ Ⓑ Ⓒ Ⓓ
115 Ⓐ Ⓑ Ⓒ Ⓓ
116 Ⓐ Ⓑ Ⓒ Ⓓ
117 Ⓐ Ⓑ Ⓒ Ⓓ
118 Ⓐ Ⓑ Ⓒ Ⓓ
119 Ⓐ Ⓑ Ⓒ Ⓓ
120 Ⓐ Ⓑ Ⓒ Ⓓ
121 Ⓐ Ⓑ Ⓒ Ⓓ
122 Ⓐ Ⓑ Ⓒ Ⓓ
123 Ⓐ Ⓑ Ⓒ Ⓓ
124 Ⓐ Ⓑ Ⓒ Ⓓ
125 Ⓐ Ⓑ Ⓒ Ⓓ
126 Ⓐ Ⓑ Ⓒ Ⓓ
127 Ⓐ Ⓑ Ⓒ Ⓓ
128 Ⓐ Ⓑ Ⓒ Ⓓ
129 Ⓐ Ⓑ Ⓒ Ⓓ
130 Ⓐ Ⓑ Ⓒ Ⓓ
131 Ⓐ Ⓑ Ⓒ Ⓓ
132 Ⓐ Ⓑ Ⓒ Ⓓ
133 Ⓐ Ⓑ Ⓒ Ⓓ
134 Ⓐ Ⓑ Ⓒ Ⓓ
135 Ⓐ Ⓑ Ⓒ Ⓓ
136 Ⓐ Ⓑ Ⓒ Ⓓ
137 Ⓐ Ⓑ Ⓒ Ⓓ
138 Ⓐ Ⓑ Ⓒ Ⓓ
139 Ⓐ Ⓑ Ⓒ Ⓓ
140 Ⓐ Ⓑ Ⓒ Ⓓ

Part VI
141 Ⓐ Ⓑ Ⓒ Ⓓ
142 Ⓐ Ⓑ Ⓒ Ⓓ
143 Ⓐ Ⓑ Ⓒ Ⓓ
144 Ⓐ Ⓑ Ⓒ Ⓓ
145 Ⓐ Ⓑ Ⓒ Ⓓ
146 Ⓐ Ⓑ Ⓒ Ⓓ
147 Ⓐ Ⓑ Ⓒ Ⓓ
148 Ⓐ Ⓑ Ⓒ Ⓓ
149 Ⓐ Ⓑ Ⓒ Ⓓ
150 Ⓐ Ⓑ Ⓒ Ⓓ
151 Ⓐ Ⓑ Ⓒ Ⓓ
152 Ⓐ Ⓑ Ⓒ Ⓓ
153 Ⓐ Ⓑ Ⓒ Ⓓ
154 Ⓐ Ⓑ Ⓒ Ⓓ
155 Ⓐ Ⓑ Ⓒ Ⓓ
156 Ⓐ Ⓑ Ⓒ Ⓓ
157 Ⓐ Ⓑ Ⓒ Ⓓ
158 Ⓐ Ⓑ Ⓒ Ⓓ
159 Ⓐ Ⓑ Ⓒ Ⓓ
160 Ⓐ Ⓑ Ⓒ Ⓓ

Part VII
161 Ⓐ Ⓑ Ⓒ Ⓓ
162 Ⓐ Ⓑ Ⓒ Ⓓ
163 Ⓐ Ⓑ Ⓒ Ⓓ
164 Ⓐ Ⓑ Ⓒ Ⓓ
165 Ⓐ Ⓑ Ⓒ Ⓓ
166 Ⓐ Ⓑ Ⓒ Ⓓ
167 Ⓐ Ⓑ Ⓒ Ⓓ
168 Ⓐ Ⓑ Ⓒ Ⓓ
169 Ⓐ Ⓑ Ⓒ Ⓓ
170 Ⓐ Ⓑ Ⓒ Ⓓ
171 Ⓐ Ⓑ Ⓒ Ⓓ
172 Ⓐ Ⓑ Ⓒ Ⓓ
173 Ⓐ Ⓑ Ⓒ Ⓓ
174 Ⓐ Ⓑ Ⓒ Ⓓ
175 Ⓐ Ⓑ Ⓒ Ⓓ
176 Ⓐ Ⓑ Ⓒ Ⓓ
177 Ⓐ Ⓑ Ⓒ Ⓓ
178 Ⓐ Ⓑ Ⓒ Ⓓ
179 Ⓐ Ⓑ Ⓒ Ⓓ
180 Ⓐ Ⓑ Ⓒ Ⓓ
181 Ⓐ Ⓑ Ⓒ Ⓓ
182 Ⓐ Ⓑ Ⓒ Ⓓ
183 Ⓐ Ⓑ Ⓒ Ⓓ
184 Ⓐ Ⓑ Ⓒ Ⓓ
185 Ⓐ Ⓑ Ⓒ Ⓓ
186 Ⓐ Ⓑ Ⓒ Ⓓ
187 Ⓐ Ⓑ Ⓒ Ⓓ
188 Ⓐ Ⓑ Ⓒ Ⓓ
189 Ⓐ Ⓑ Ⓒ Ⓓ
190 Ⓐ Ⓑ Ⓒ Ⓓ
191 Ⓐ Ⓑ Ⓒ Ⓓ
192 Ⓐ Ⓑ Ⓒ Ⓓ
193 Ⓐ Ⓑ Ⓒ Ⓓ
194 Ⓐ Ⓑ Ⓒ Ⓓ
195 Ⓐ Ⓑ Ⓒ Ⓓ
196 Ⓐ Ⓑ Ⓒ Ⓓ
197 Ⓐ Ⓑ Ⓒ Ⓓ
198 Ⓐ Ⓑ Ⓒ Ⓓ
199 Ⓐ Ⓑ Ⓒ Ⓓ
200 Ⓐ Ⓑ Ⓒ Ⓓ

Answer Sheet Practice Test 2

Listening Comprehension

Part I	Part II	Part III	Part IV
1 (A)(B)(C)(D)	21 (A)(B)(C)	51 (A)(B)(C)(D)	81 (A)(B)(C)(D)
2 (A)(B)(C)(D)	22 (A)(B)(C)	52 (A)(B)(C)(D)	82 (A)(B)(C)(D)
3 (A)(B)(C)(D)	23 (A)(B)(C)	53 (A)(B)(C)(D)	83 (A)(B)(C)(D)
4 (A)(B)(C)(D)	24 (A)(B)(C)	54 (A)(B)(C)(D)	84 (A)(B)(C)(D)
5 (A)(B)(C)(D)	25 (A)(B)(C)	55 (A)(B)(C)(D)	85 (A)(B)(C)(D)
6 (A)(B)(C)(D)	26 (A)(B)(C)	56 (A)(B)(C)(D)	86 (A)(B)(C)(D)
7 (A)(B)(C)(D)	27 (A)(B)(C)	57 (A)(B)(C)(D)	87 (A)(B)(C)(D)
8 (A)(B)(C)(D)	28 (A)(B)(C)	58 (A)(B)(C)(D)	88 (A)(B)(C)(D)
9 (A)(B)(C)(D)	29 (A)(B)(C)	59 (A)(B)(C)(D)	89 (A)(B)(C)(D)
10 (A)(B)(C)(D)	30 (A)(B)(C)	60 (A)(B)(C)(D)	90 (A)(B)(C)(D)
11 (A)(B)(C)(D)	31 (A)(B)(C)	61 (A)(B)(C)(D)	91 (A)(B)(C)(D)
12 (A)(B)(C)(D)	32 (A)(B)(C)	62 (A)(B)(C)(D)	92 (A)(B)(C)(D)
13 (A)(B)(C)(D)	33 (A)(B)(C)	63 (A)(B)(C)(D)	93 (A)(B)(C)(D)
14 (A)(B)(C)(D)	34 (A)(B)(C)	64 (A)(B)(C)(D)	94 (A)(B)(C)(D)
15 (A)(B)(C)(D)	35 (A)(B)(C)	65 (A)(B)(C)(D)	95 (A)(B)(C)(D)
16 (A)(B)(C)(D)	36 (A)(B)(C)	66 (A)(B)(C)(D)	96 (A)(B)(C)(D)
17 (A)(B)(C)(D)	37 (A)(B)(C)	67 (A)(B)(C)(D)	97 (A)(B)(C)(D)
18 (A)(B)(C)(D)	38 (A)(B)(C)	68 (A)(B)(C)(D)	98 (A)(B)(C)(D)
19 (A)(B)(C)(D)	39 (A)(B)(C)	69 (A)(B)(C)(D)	99 (A)(B)(C)(D)
20 (A)(B)(C)(D)	40 (A)(B)(C)	70 (A)(B)(C)(D)	100 (A)(B)(C)(D)
	41 (A)(B)(C)	71 (A)(B)(C)(D)	
	42 (A)(B)(C)	72 (A)(B)(C)(D)	
	43 (A)(B)(C)	73 (A)(B)(C)(D)	
	44 (A)(B)(C)	74 (A)(B)(C)(D)	
	45 (A)(B)(C)	75 (A)(B)(C)(D)	
	46 (A)(B)(C)	76 (A)(B)(C)(D)	
	47 (A)(B)(C)	77 (A)(B)(C)(D)	
	48 (A)(B)(C)	78 (A)(B)(C)(D)	
	49 (A)(B)(C)	79 (A)(B)(C)(D)	
	50 (A)(B)(C)	80 (A)(B)(C)(D)	

Reading

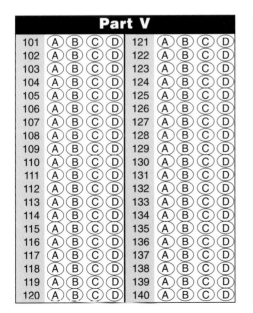

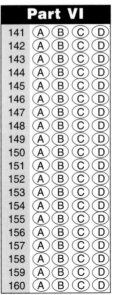

Part V — 101–140 (A)(B)(C)(D)

Part VI — 141–160 (A)(B)(C)(D)

Part VII — 161–200 (A)(B)(C)(D)

Practice Test Conversion Table

Match the number of correct answers with the corresponding Practice Score.
Add the two Practice scores together. This is your estimated total Practice Score.

Number Correct Listening = Listening Practice Score _____

Number Correct Reading = Reading Practice Score + _____

Total estimated Practice Score _____

Practice Test Estimated Conversion Table

Number Correct	Listening Practice Score	Reading Practice Score	Number Correct	Listening Practice Score	Reading Practice Score
0	5	5	51	255	220
1	5	5	52	260	225
2	5	5	53	270	230
3	5	5	54	275	235
4	5	5	55	280	240
5	5	5	56	290	250
6	5	5	57	295	255
7	10	5	58	300	260
8	15	5	59	310	265
9	20	5	60	315	270
10	25	5	61	320	280
11	30	5	62	325	285
12	35	5	63	330	290
13	40	5	64	340	300
14	45	5	65	345	305
15	50	5	66	350	310
16	55	10	67	360	320
17	60	15	68	365	325
18	65	20	69	370	330
19	70	25	70	380	335
20	75	30	71	385	340
21	80	35	72	390	350
22	85	40	73	395	355
23	90	45	74	400	360
24	95	50	75	405	365
25	100	60	76	410	370
26	110	65	77	420	380
27	115	70	78	425	385
28	120	80	79	430	390
29	125	85	80	440	395
30	130	90	81	445	400
31	135	95	82	450	405
32	140	100	83	460	410
33	145	110	84	465	415
34	150	115	85	470	420
35	160	120	86	475	425
36	165	125	87	480	430
37	170	130	88	485	435
38	175	140	89	490	445
39	180	145	90	495	450
40	185	150	91	495	455
41	190	160	92	495	465
42	195	165	93	495	470
43	200	170	94	495	480
44	210	175	95	495	485
45	215	180	96	495	490
46	220	190	97	495	495
47	230	195	98	495	495
48	240	200	99	495	495
49	245	210	100	495	495
50	250	215			